SUMMER MADNESS

SUMMER MADNESS

HOW BREXIT SPLIT THE TORIES, DESTROYED LABOUR AND DIVIDED THE COUNTRY

HARRY MOUNT

Biteback Publishing

First published in Great Britain in 2017 by
Biteback Publishing Ltd
Westminster Tower
3 Albert Embankment
London SE1 7SP

ISBN 978-1-78590-179-9

10 9 8 7 6 5 4 3 2 1

A CIP catalogue record for this book is available from the British Library.

Set in Minion

Printed and bound in Great Britain by
CPI Group (UK) Ltd, Croydon CR0 4YY

To the late Angus Macintyre, in homage and affection

CONTENTS

A NATIONAL BLOODBATH

Shortly after Michael Gove knifed Boris Johnson front, back and sideways, a close friend of Boris's said, white-faced, to me, 'Brexit is like some horrible curse. It kills everything it touches.'

In less than three weeks – from the referendum vote on 23 June to Theresa May's elevation to Prime Minister on 13 July – Brexit morphed into a mass murderer.

Now the boil has been partly lanced, the anger of those days has largely dissipated. But then, the scent of slaughter, and the attendant panic, were everywhere, on the streets of Westminster and beyond. It was like one of those arcing power cables, leaping all over a petrol station drowning in slicks of fuel, torching every surface it came into contact with. The sparking cable even went lashing through the High Court and the Supreme Court, as they ruled that Parliament must approve Brexit – and were given a thorough going-over by the press in return.

The Bullingdon boys – David Cameron and George

Osborne – had been whacked. The Cabinet was drained of blue blood – 22 per cent of May's reshuffled Cabinet were public-school educated, compared to 45 per cent of Cameron's. May herself morphed into a hardline Brexiteer, as her red-blooded Lancaster House speech on 17 January 2017 revealed.

The Notting Hill Set – who had holidayed, worked and lived together for thirty years since their Oxford days – were also torn asunder by the Brexit serial killer. Michael Gove and Boris Johnson – who had fought the Brexit campaign, who had broken bread and plotted together alongside their wives – were ripped apart by Gove's sudden desertion. Gove's principal ally, Nick Boles, who had also deserted Boris on the night before his leadership launch, was also destroyed by his own fatal lack of loyalty.

Even Jeremy Corbyn, the lone big beast who remained in post before and after the referendum, joined the ranks of the living dead. Shortly after the Brexit result, Labour MPs voted against him, 172–40, in a no-confidence vote. Over the course of two days, twenty-three out of thirty-one of his shadow Cabinet resigned. In the Richmond Park by-election in December 2016, Labour got 1,515 votes, 3.7 per cent of the vote. They lost their deposit – the first time the party has lost its deposit in a London by-election for a century. In the Slea-ford and North Hykeham by-election a week later, Labour came fourth, with a 7.1 per cent swing against them.

And the only real victor of the referendum, Nigel Farage, was evaporated by his own success, resigning his UKIP leadership within days of the referendum; even if he did return, yet again, briefly, as interim leader, and as Donald Trump's de facto ambassador to the United Kingdom.

In Farage's view, even Trump's victory was thanks, in part, to Brexit.

'Everybody around Trump was saying the impetus of Brexit was crucial,' says Farage. 'It inspired the door-knockers and the leaflet deliverers, and non-voters in particular – they thought, if it can happen in Britain, it can happen anywhere.'

Matteo Renzi's referendum loss in Italy in December can't be attributed to Brexit – but, still, it was part and parcel of a year of revolution. If not as big as 1848 – the Year of Revolution, when over fifty countries were hit by political upheaval – 2016 was the most chaotic political year of the modern era.

I have been a journalist since 2000. I have covered four general elections. I saw Alastair Campbell at his most power-crazed, puppeteering Tony Blair around the streets of Uxbridge with a tiny flicker of his right index finger. I witnessed the defenestration of Iain Duncan Smith; the nervous anger of Gordon Brown. I heard Peter Mandelson damn David Cameron with his most withering of putdowns.

'When I said that Cameron looks down his long toffee nose at people, it was just witty repartee, a bit of a tease; I'm hardly one to talk myself,' said Mandelson, wrinkling that elongated nose of his with a mocking grin, straight out of the Prince of Darkness Book of Menacing Looks.

But I have never seen such viciousness, anger, madness, plot and counterplot as I did in the build-up to the referendum – all of it doubled and redoubled in the immediate aftermath.

Just as the country had a sort of collective breakdown over the referendum, so did high politics. The schism wasn't just political; it was also emotional, spiritual and intellectual.

Politics is famously a ruthless, nasty game. I had never seen it so ruthless or so nasty.

The following pages give an insider's tale of those three chilling weeks of mass blood-letting – and explain how the various, squabbling Brexit groups dallied with mutual destruction before pulling off the biggest political coup of the century – that is, until it was trumped, just over four months later, in America.

They also answer the two big questions of the summer madness of 2016. Why did Michael Gove knife Boris Johnson so late? And why did Boris decide to stand down once he'd been knifed? He is hardly backward in coming forward – as a little boy, he declared his ambition was to be 'world king'.

Yes, he was severely wounded by Gove's knife blow, but he was still very much alive, and backed to the hilt by many significant supporters, aggrieved at the manner of his assassination. Why did he wimp out?

At the time, I talked to many of the principal combatants, as I wrote articles for the *Evening Standard*, *The Spectator* and the *Sunday Times*. The volume of bile sloshing back and forth between the different factions of the Conservative Party was astonishing. After Gove destroyed Johnson, leading figures in the Boris camp said they wanted to destroy Gove for his disloyalty. In the end, it wasn't just Gove who was destroyed. The referendum led to the most brutal act of political hara-kiri in modern British history – bloodthirsty even by Tory leadership standards.

How had it all ended up like this, with these three weeks of the long knives that left a whole political generation dead and buried?

It had all started five years earlier, in the Tate Britain gallery, by the Thames, where a small ginger group of Eurosceptic politicians gathered on an informal, regular basis, with one intention in mind – to get Britain out of the EU.

None of them thought they'd be quite so spectacularly successful – and quite so quickly.

CHAPTER 1

THE TATE BRITAIN PLOT
– OR HOW TO FORCE A
REFERENDUM

There's nowhere to eat in the culinary desert that is Westminster. That's the traditional cry of MPs and political journalists, who never take the short stroll down the Thames to Tate Britain – home to the best collection of British art in the country.

Tate Britain also has a charming restaurant, lined with a Rex Whistler mural, 'The Expedition in Pursuit of Rare Meats', described by the architectural historian Sir Nikolaus Pevsner as 'fey, nostalgic, mural capricci'.

It was in that restaurant that the exit of Britain from the EU was planned by a tiny cadre of Eurosceptics.

The three regular members of the group that began meeting in 2011 were Daniel Hannan, a Tory MEP for South East England, Douglas Carswell, the Tory MP and later UKIP MP for Clacton, and Mark Reckless, the Tory MP for Rochester and Strood, who defected to UKIP in 2014, losing his seat at the following general election.

'We'd usually meet at Tate Britain,' says Hannan, forty-five. 'Sometimes in that gorgeous Rex Whistler restaurant with the murals, sometimes in the café, sometimes just walking around the pictures. We guessed that we'd never meet any MPs or hacks there, and we never did.'

It just goes to show that MPs, and journalists, must be very incurious, or lacking in an artistic hinterland, or so unable to escape the Westminster bubble at its smallest, that they never venture into neighbouring Pimlico.

Chief among the Tate Britain Group was Hannan – who had been at Marlborough and Oxford with Reckless and had written, with Carswell, *The Plan: Twelve Months to Renew Britain*, in 2008. The book argued for a radical decentralisation and democratisation of power, through a combination of self-financing councils, open primaries for political candidates and an elected Senate of the Regions instead of the House of Lords. It also demanded more local and national referendums.

From 1999, Hannan has been a Member of the European Parliament, determined to bring down the institution he works for, exposing the perils of the euro, even though he was hated for saying so. MEPs used to turn their backs on him in the lifts in Brussels, for exposing the rackets they were cashing in on – like the classic scam of charging expenses for a full-fare ticket from Brussels to the UK, taking a budget flight and pocketing the difference.

I must declare an interest. I worked with Hannan at the *Daily Telegraph* as a fellow leader-writer from 2000 to 2005, and he is a friend of mine.

When I started in journalism, working with Hannan on the comment pages of the *Daily Telegraph* in 2000, I was given two rules:

1. Never publish a piece by an MP – they're always boring.
2. Never publish a piece on the EU – they're always boring.

Seventeen years on, rule number one remains true. Rule number two has become dramatically, viciously, grippingly untrue.

Hannan once took me on an afternoon tour of the European Parliament, exposing its vast expenditure. At one moment, on a whim, he threw open an anonymous-looking door in an obscure passage. On the other side, a full orchestra was playing Beethoven's 'Ode to Joy' – the European Union anthem.

'They're always in there, practising for evening receptions,' Hannan said, chuckling.

Later on in his tour, he showed me a huge, hideous steel sculpture of interlocking tubes that reached from the basement of the Parliament right up to its highest rafters. With a vigorous push, he set the whole thing a-jangling. And it just kept on jangling.

'It goes on for about five minutes,' he said, as a security guard approached him.

'Did you see who did that?' said the guard.

'No idea,' said Hannan, adopting a serious expression on his cherubic features, 'So sorry.'

Hannan's mischief belies the seriousness of his mission – to get Britain out of the EU – a mission he set out on while still a teenager at Oxford.

Before then, he'd had an extraordinary childhood. Born in Peru, he saw his Second World War veteran father's plantation taken away by a military government in the 1970s.

This, more than anything, defines his political outlook. I remember at one *Telegraph* leader conference when the Blair government suggested confiscating any second home that hadn't been occupied for more than twelve years. All the leader-writers attacked the idea – and it never materialised in the end – but Hannan was particularly exercised.

'You soft lot brought up in Britain don't realise that this is what governments can do,' he said.

It's striking that Douglas Carswell, too, was brought up abroad, the son of doctors working in Uganda. Just as Hannan was politicised by Peruvian revolution, so Carswell's libertarian politics were created by Idi Amin's tyrannical regime. Boris Johnson was born in New York; a big chunk of his childhood was spent in Brussels; he is a quarter Turkish. He should really be called Boris Kemal. His paternal great-grandfather was Ali Kemal, an Ottoman journalist and Minister of the Interior, murdered in 1922 in the Turkish War of Independence.

'People call Eurosceptics nativist, Little Englanders,' says

Carswell, 'but it's because we've seen the world that we know what goes wrong with uncontrolled government power.'

I was at Oxford at the same time as Hannan. I didn't know him but I knew of him: he was already a public personality at the university, cropping up in the gossip column of *Cherwell* as a prominent Tory. At the end of his first term, in winter 1990, he set up an Oxford chapter of the Eurosceptic group Campaign for an Independent Britain, with Mark Reckless.

He had become a figure of right-wing legend, organising protests against Jacques Delors, the President of the European Commission, when we were at Oxford in the early '90s. In one stunt, Hannan and several allies plastered posters, advertising Delors' speaker meetings at Oxford, with a 'Cancelled' banner, with the effective intention of keeping audience numbers down.

In another stunt, to protest against the Maastricht Treaty of 1992, Hannan and other Oxford Eurosceptics 'doughnutted' Norman Lamont, then Chancellor of the Exchequer, at a Europhile meeting in Bath – that is, they surrounded him, to give the impression to the television cameras that there were many more protesters than there actually were.

It was Maastricht, which created the EU out of the EEC, and enshrined further European integration, that galvanised Hannan, Carswell and Reckless, all born in 1970 or 1971.

'The 1975 referendum extinguished Euroscepticism for a generation. After a two-to-one vote to stay in, it was over,' says Hannan. 'It was Maastricht that got things going again.'

It was Maastricht, too, that galvanised the group of Eurosceptic MPs to fight John Major.

'We realised then that there was collusion over Europe between the two front benches, government and the whips,' says veteran Eurosceptic MP Sir Bill Cash. 'So, day by day, we had to engage in operational activities to outwit them, right the way from Maastricht onwards.'

By 2011, when the Tate Britain Group started to meet, the European issue had come to a head. In March 2011, the People's Pledge – a campaign calling on voters to support MPs who backed an EU referendum – was launched. In October 2011, the Tory MP David Nuttall proposed a motion for an EU referendum. Although the motion was defeated by 483 to 111, at least eighty-one Tory MPs defied the whip, the biggest ever rebellion against a Tory Prime Minister over Europe. The Commons debate was prompted by a petition signed by more than 100,000 people.

The pressure for Cameron to hold a referendum increased when it became clear that UKIP wouldn't do a deal to stand down in seats where they threatened Tories. At this stage, it was becoming clear that UKIP might constitute a serious electoral threat to the Tories at the next election.

'Mark Reckless drew up a paper to see whether a deal could be done, so as not to stand against each other,' says Chris Bruni-Lowe, Nigel Farage's campaign director. 'But Nigel Farage said it wasn't Marquess of Queensberry rules [to do deals like that].'

Increasingly, David Cameron began to think the best way

to shoot UKIP's fox was to hold a referendum. From 2011 onwards, the Eurosceptics had pushed for a referendum and, on 23 January 2013, they seemed to have their moment.

On that day, Cameron in his 'Bloomberg speech' – held at the Bloomberg HQ in London – said he was keen on reforming Europe and that he would hold a referendum if the Tories won the next election.

The seeds of the referendum had been planted in a pizza restaurant at Chicago's O'Hare airport on 21 May 2012. Returning from a NATO summit, David Cameron ate in the restaurant with William Hague, the Foreign Secretary, and Ed Llewellyn, Cameron's chief of staff. Over their pizzas, they agreed it was time to have an EU referendum.

George Osborne advised against it. He was opposed to referendums in general because they rarely ended up being about the subject on the ballot paper; instead, they sucked in any general discontent in the air.

And the new book that Osborne is writing, *The Age of Unreason*, suggests that there's a lot of discontent about; that capitalism and democracy are in crisis, and populist nationalism and prejudice are increasing, amplified by new technology. In the old days, a populist agenda on, say, immigration would be challenged by the BBC news in the evening. Now it's echoed back on social media. Thus, politics is pushed to its extremes in Germany, France and in America, in the form of Donald Trump.

'It's still different in general elections,' says a senior adviser to George Osborne. 'The first-past-the-post system entrenches the power of established parties. So UKIP got 4 million votes and only one MP at the general election. You don't get that effect in a referendum.'

In such a climate, thought Osborne, it was not a good idea to take a gamble on a referendum which aggregated so many bubbling issues: the government, the NHS, immigration and parliamentary sovereignty chief among them. The referendum loss that brought down Matteo Renzi in December 2016 was fatal for a similar reason. Unlike Cameron, the Italian Prime Minister tied his own resignation to a referendum loss – and so the referendum acted as a magnet for any voter dissatisfied with Renzi's administration.

The situation wasn't helped by Osborne's Omnishambles budget in April 2012 – with the lambasted pasty tax, charity tax, churches tax and caravan tax. And then, in October 2012, came the rebellion by fifty-three Tory MPs – on a motion demanding a cut in the EU budget. The pressure grew too great.

'Cameron's very aware that the mood of the Conservative Party is only shifting one way,' recalls Carswell. 'It's partly the success of tactics in Parliament, partly what's going on in the Eurozone. They may have got wind of a series of by-elections [caused by Tory MPs defecting to UKIP, as Carswell and Reckless would eventually do in 2014]. We were toying with that idea before Bloomberg.'

To begin with, the Tate Britain Group were happy with the outcome.

'What Cameron said at Bloomberg was superb, spot on,' says Carswell. '[But] it turns out that what was promised

– the fundamental change of our relationship with Europe – he didn't mean it. He's talking about change within the European Union, not change that applies exclusively to the UK, to our relationship with the EU. Bloomberg was a pig in a poke.'

And so the Tate Britain Group went into overdrive. They had achieved their first objective – to get David Cameron to give them a referendum.

'The other objective was to make sure Nigel [Farage] and some of the more passionate advocates didn't lose us the referendum,' says Carswell.

Therein lies what has been called the Farage Paradox: the more the support for UKIP went up, the less inclined non-UKIP supporters were to advocate leaving the European Union. In other words, the success of Farage among his heartland voters put off moderate voters in the middle ground.

This led to one of the great echoes of *that* scene in *Monty Python's Life of Brian* – where the People's Front of Judea loathe the Judean People's Front:

REG: The only people we hate more than the Romans are the fucking Judean People's Front.
PEOPLE'S FRONT OF JUDEA: Yeah…
JUDITH: Splitters.
PFJ: Splitters…
FRANCIS: And the Judean Popular People's Front.
PFJ: Yeah. Oh, yeah. Splitters. Splitters…
LORETTA: And the People's Front of Judea.

PFJ: Yeah. Splitters. Splitters…

REG: What?

LORETTA: The People's Front of Judea. Splitters.

REG: We're the People's Front of Judea!

LORETTA: Oh. I thought we were the Popular Front.

REG: People's Front! Chuh.

FRANCIS: Whatever happened to the Popular Front, Reg?

REG: He's over there.

PFJ: Splitter!

The Monty Python scene ridiculed the differences between hard-left groupings in 1970s Britain.

The differences still linger on today. At a Jeremy Corbyn rally in Parliament Square on 27 June 2016 – four days after the referendum – I saw a poster that went right against the Europhile spirit of the gathering: 'Down with the EU! For a workers [sic] Europe! Spartacist.'

But the biggest hatred in the referendum campaign wasn't between Remainers and Brexiteers. It was between Nigel Farage and the leaders of Vote Leave.

The other splinter groups for Leave had problems with each other, too. Because Eurosceptics have so often been voices in the wilderness, calling in vain for their cause, they have often hardened into loners. When called upon to coalesce, they found it difficult – not least when the long-term Eurosceptic MPs, such as Sir Bill Cash and Bernard Jenkin, were confronted with fly-by-night Eurosceptics, like Boris Johnson. Those veterans admired the intellect of Douglas Carswell and

Daniel Hannan, but also looked at them as prima donnas who had never done enough for the cause as a team effort.

But the real hate figure for Vote Leave was Nigel Farage.

'We had been looking at polling data and we'd seen the Farage Paradox,' says Carswell. 'It was the thing that most troubled us. Often, great reformist movements have, at key moments, advocates who are offensive to the undecided.'

The need to take on the Farage Paradox was crucial in the Brexit campaign. It explains why Dominic Cummings and Matthew Elliott, who led Vote Leave, were determined that the various Brexit groups shouldn't coalesce – because, they said, Nigel Farage would become too prominent; and if he became too prominent, Cummings, Elliott and the Tate Britain Group were convinced Brexit would fail.

After Elliott was appointed chief executive of Vote Leave, Dominic Cummings was appointed campaign director.

Cummings, forty-five, is an uncompromising figure – political Marmite. His opponents utterly loathe him; his supporters venerate his Jedi mastery of political tactics. 'Dominic was pretty determined to be unaccountable and it was a constant battle,' says Bernard Jenkin MP, a founding director of Vote Leave who fell out with Cummings. 'He has a very creative mind and finds it very difficult to work with people who disagree with him.' David Cameron called Cummings a 'career psychopath', while Daniel Hannan says, 'Matt asked me what I thought of appointing Dominic Cummings as campaign director. I told him that it was his call but, as far as I was concerned, Dom was the best street-fighter around.'

'A lot of feathers were ruffled by Dom, but he had to,' says Douglas Carswell.

In any event, people will come in like that Harry Enfield character and say, 'You don't want to do it like this, you want to do it like that.'

There was creative tension between Dominic and others, but that's how innovations happen. You don't create something without difference of opinion and sparks flying.

'I'd known Dominic for many years,' says Matthew Elliott.

He'd done a huge amount of polling for Business for Britain after the 2014 European elections, which really formed the basis for a lot of our thinking for Vote Leave about where public opinion was, about taking control, about how to deal with the migration issue, about how to deal with the status quo, with Remain being the safer option. All that thinking was done by him around then. We did more research after the election but already a lot of it had been done.

Dom is a fearless fighter, brilliant at running a war room, great strategic brain, absolutely first class.

After getting a First in Ancient and Modern History at Oxford in 1994, Cummings was campaign director for Business for Sterling, dedicated to stopping Britain joining the euro. For eight months in 2002, he was director of strategy for Iain Duncan Smith. I once saw him in action in that post at a dinner for prospective Conservative parliamentary candidates in the House of Commons.

One after another, these fresh-faced figures talked up the prospects of the Tories, and their own electoral prospects, too.

And, one after another, Cummings told them: 'You don't stand a chance… You don't stand a chance… You don't stand a chance…' With the Tories then at their nadir, and Tony Blair's New Labour at its zenith, he was spot on.

In 2004, Cummings masterminded the campaign against a North-East Regional Assembly, as proposed by John Prescott, then Deputy Prime Minister. Cummings, himself from Durham, prevailed, in part thanks to another simple but effective stunt: an inflatable white elephant, which toured the north-east in the build-up to the vote. The result – 77.9 per cent no to 22.1 per cent yes – was resounding.

From 2007 to 2014, Cummings worked as an adviser to Michael Gove, first in opposition and then when Gove was Education Secretary.

In the flesh – well, there isn't much flesh – Cummings is a spare, ascetic man, indifferent to smart clothes and to what people think of him. Once when I was fishing for some political gossip from him, he said, 'I don't know and, if I did know, I wouldn't tell you.'

He is exceptionally intelligent, absorbing huge amounts of information, analysing it surgically and then coming to solid conclusions that he doggedly sticks by. He is immune to criticism – hatred, even – which meant he was a crucial ally of Gove's when they were taking on the combined forces of 'the Blob', the education Establishment, which opposed the reforming measures of Gove and Cummings. If Gove had ended up as Chancellor alongside Boris as Prime Minister, the plan was that Cummings would take on the great post-war challenge of government – reforming the civil service.

As a result of Cummings's high intelligence and remorseless ability to take on any opposition, Gove – himself very clever and confident about that intelligence – defers to Cummings as his ultimate adviser. Boris, too, has a correctly high opinion of his own gifts – but also deferred to the Cummings planet brain during the referendum campaign.

Cummings is perfectly happy – perhaps happiest – working on his own. I happened to bump into him in the autumn of 2015, just as the Vote Leave campaign was launched. He was having coffee outside the Tomtom Coffee House on Ebury Street, Victoria, tapping away on his laptop. I had heard rumours about him heading up the new campaign.

'Where is the Vote Leave office?' I asked.

'This is the Vote Leave office,' he said, pointing at his laptop.

Cummings is convinced that it 'would have been a complete disaster' to merge campaigns with Nigel Farage and Arron Banks.

'We would have lost badly,' Cummings says, 'They're out-of-control people. Anybody good at Vote Leave would have walked out, thinking, "I don't want this on my CV."'

Cummings also thinks that, without Farage, they would have won the referendum by a bigger margin.

'If Farage had retired in May 2015, we would have got 55 per cent,' says Cummings, 'If we could have dropped Bernard Jenkin, we could have got 60 per cent.'

Most of the Vote Leave team accept, however, that a more moderate Farage might have boosted the Leave vote.

'The tragedy was that, before the 2015 election, Farage said he'd go round the northern cities,' says Cummings. 'If he'd stuck to that, it would have been very useful.'

The computer experts recruited by Cummings had ranked 10,000 British postcodes by electoral profile.

'They ranked them with the probability of being on our side, which proved to be remarkably accurate,' says Cummings, 'We knew exactly where to send Farage. I offered him the list to turn out the vote.'

'He said, "That's very interesting, Dominic. What about the BBC debates?"'

Cummings wasn't entirely opposed to Farage at the beginning of the campaign, however.

The Farage Paradox is not correct. The more people were thinking about immigration, the better for us. There's a group of people for whom Farage is persuasive and motivating. It's not true to say Farage is a disaster for the whole thing.

But, as he starts to go mad, on Putin, and HIV, that's motivating for, say, 20–25 per cent, but anti-motivating for another group of people. That's the core problem. The people he's motivating are all going to vote for us. To win, you've got to get 50 per cent.

It was also the Farage Paradox that prompted Douglas Carswell to defect from the Conservatives to join UKIP on 28 August 2014 – taking a bullet, as Daniel Hannan puts it.

'These Tate Gallery discussions continue,' says Carswell. 'We've got to ramp up the pressure to get a referendum; and we think we can see that coming but we can't be sure. And I do what I did on 28 August 2014, to help do that. I'd been toying with the idea for a long time.'

Carswell's defection – and that of Mark Reckless, MP for Rochester and Strood – were coordinated by Chris Bruni-Lowe. He had once worked as a private pollster for the Tories, before becoming director of Nigel Farage's referendum campaign. Young, good-looking, fashionably dressed, shaven-headed, he is not cut from the stereotypical UKIP cloth – but he is extremely close to Farage, and instrumental in his political thinking.

'Reckless wanted to defect at the beginning of 2014, at the time of the European elections,' says Bruni-Lowe.

He thought that the longer he had as a UKIP MP, the better his chances of winning at the general election. But he was dissuaded, because he wasn't getting the Labour voters he needed.

Carswell then said to Reckless, 'I want to defect,' and I helped devise his strategy. Reckless and I planned Carswell's defection. I thought, I can't work with this bloke. He's a complete nutcase, he's crazy, he's awful, he's not very nice. Reckless said, 'No – hang on in there.'

When Carswell defected to UKIP, he also resigned his seat as an MP – something he wasn't obliged to do – and triggered a by-election. He won that by-election on 9 October 2014, with a majority of 12,404.

Carswell was traduced by some as a far-right-wing nutter, an opinion boosted by his ungainly manner. He is six foot four, balding, with an oddly angled lower jaw that moves in a different universe from the rest of his skull. Only forty-five, he speaks in old-fashioned, received English and is given to military metaphors. In other words, a walking Tory Boy stereotype. The Eurosceptics had always been mocked for their odd looks – until they won.

In fact, Carswell is to the left of the Conservative Party, his main cause is libertarianism and, in our interview in Portcullis House, often says he is horrified with UKIP.

'Up until the end of 2014, UKIP were a minority, acquired taste,' Carswell says. 'But it wasn't quite the repulsive, electorally toxic brand that it was to become: comments about HIV, breastfeeding in public…'

Carswell refuses to name Farage at this point, but it was Farage who, in December 2014, said women should breastfeed in a corner; Farage who, in October 2014, said immigrants with HIV should be kept out of Britain. That particularly riled Carswell – whose father, Dr Wilson Carswell, diagnosed the first Ugandan case of AIDS in the early 1980s. Dr Carswell also inspired the character of Dr Nicholas Garrigan in Giles Foden's novel *The Last King of Scotland*, later turned into a film.

So Carswell didn't move to UKIP as a rightward step. He did it with one view in mind: to get a referendum that would take Britain out of the EU.

'It's the reason I'm in politics,' he says. 'I've been campaigning to leave the EU since 1993. I joined UKIP for the same reason I joined the Conservative Party – I thought it was the most effective vehicle to get us out of the European Union.'

One of Carswell's principal aims, too, was to solve the Farage Paradox – to detoxify the UKIP brand.

'I'm desperate that Nigel shouldn't lead the Leave campaign,' he says.

By joining UKIP, I hope that one can detoxify it.

This is Euroscepticism's long-standing problem. It was always fought by people who fought a long retreat, precisely because they talked about sovereignty and immigration and the constitution – things that really wound up people who already believed in what the Bruges Group [a Eurosceptic group] were saying.

The need to secure a referendum and to get Britain out of Europe also explains Mark Reckless's defection to UKIP on 27 September 2014. He, too, resigned his seat and triggered a by-election on 20 November 2014, which he won by a majority of 2,920.

By September, Nigel Farage knew Mark Reckless was defecting and he wanted to time it for the UKIP conference of 26–27 September; but also to coincide his defection with the moment postal votes were sent out for Carswell's by-election in October, so that UKIP would be on the front pages of the papers.

The UKIP plan was to keep attracting Tory defectors, one by one, to pile the pressure on Cameron.

'I polled for Adam Holloway and Philip Hollobone [Conservative MPs for Gravesham and Kettering, respectively] in their constituency, asking if you're more likely to vote for your MP [if they stood for UKIP],' says Chris Bruni-Lowe, Farage's chief pollster. 'Holloway polled higher than anyone else. He would have won as anything.'

The motives for the defections varied.

'Reckless's aim was to go to join UKIP,' says Bruni-Lowe.

I remember him saying to Nigel, 'You're a hero.' Carswell's defection was different. People still don't know why. Carswell wanted to detoxify it from within. Why would you join a party with Nigel as leader and immigration as the number one policy, and then complain about both?

Carswell said he wanted to do a speech, saying Enoch Powell was wrong, at the exact same time we were pushing immigration. He wanted to break UKIP up from within. He's happier, thinking they're voting for his surgeries and fish and chip suppers [rather than for UKIP's core policies]. No, they're not. Go to Clacton.

Whatever the individual motives for the defections, the two by-election victories had their intended effect.

'The pressure of those two by-elections is such that Cameron, two weeks into that Rochester by-election, has to say that he would legislate for a referendum within the first 100 days,' says Carswell, 'He had committed [to a referendum] under Bloomberg but it was vague; it was wishy-washy. He gives us a clear commitment to legislate within 100 days.'

The die was cast. The European Union Referendum Act was introduced to the Commons on 28 May 2015, passed by the Commons by six to one, and given Royal Assent on 17 December 2015. On 20 February 2016, David Cameron announced that the referendum would take place on 23 June 2016.

Despite this success, one fly in the ointment for the Brexiteers at the end of 2014 was how badly Douglas Carswell was getting on with Nigel Farage.

'We underestimated the extent to which the shock and awful tactics could be used,' says Carswell. He had always believed that Farage was a risk to the referendum. In the build-up to the 2015 general election, he began to think Farage was the biggest single risk.

By the time of the general election, I realised that trying to detoxify UKIP was a forlorn activity. Under the current leadership, there was no chance of that.

To detoxify UKIP, you need a different leader and a different tone and that's not going to happen. [Instead,] I put my effort into making sure there was a distance between a toxic brand and Vote Leave.

If a UKIP-led organisation had been in charge of the campaign, we wouldn't have even got a majority of the votes in Clacton. In Clacton, UKIP got 44 per cent of the vote – so most people in Clacton don't vote UKIP. Seventy-something per cent voted Leave. Overwhelming. These are people I know and respect, who won't vote for my party. Many tell me they hold their nose as they do so.

To win that referendum, we absolutely had to not be a UKIP-run organisation. If UKIP had toned things down, if they had not done deals with Downing Street to get on the television, quite disgracefully, for ITV to allow someone who had nothing to do with the official Out campaign [i.e. Nigel Farage] to be its spokesman, if the persistent attempts of the mainstream media to collude with portraying Nigel as the voice of Leave, we would have won 60–40.

If I were to say that Eddie Izzard should be the official spokesperson for Remain, most people would say, hang on, Izzard is no more a spokesperson than Nigel is for Leave.

Nigel Farage does not quite see things the way Douglas Carswell does.

CHAPTER 2

THE VIEW FROM NIGEL FARAGE'S SMOKING TERRACE

The devil doesn't play all the best tunes; the underdog does. Or at least that's how it worked out in the European referendum. Because the Brexiteers were considered the outsiders, they had to work that much harder – and with that much smaller a cast of characters.

UKIP's former office on Great Smith Street, a few paces from Westminster Abbey, is a case in point. It's a handsome enough, but hardly grand, eighteenth-century, classical brick townhouse. Inside, it's cramped and surprisingly small – a Tardis in reverse.

The Westminster bubble and the Westminster village may be clichés, but that doesn't mean those clichés are incorrect. The cast of characters at Westminster is extremely small – spend enough time hanging around as a journalist, even on the fringes, and you soon come across most of the leading political characters.

Just in the course of researching this book, I bumped into David Cameron, having a farewell drink with his special advisers in a St James's wine bar – he was on the beer, incidentally. Having lunch with Cleo Watson, the Vote Leave head of outreach, in Orso, a Covent Garden restaurant, Michael Gove was sitting two tables down from us.

A small world... Still, I was surprised by quite how small the UKIP operation was: a bank of eight computer terminals on one long desk, each with its own swivel chair in front of it. From these eight desks, the UKIP leadership orchestrated its nationwide campaign, with the added help of a young secretary, Vicky, who booked the buses for the rallies.

When I visited the office on 1 September 2016, it was empty, except for Vicky, Gawain Towler, the UKIP head of press, two young men sitting at the row of desks – and Farage himself.

Gone were the thick-set security men who often accompanied Farage on the campaign trail. Three or four of them followed him at most events, after death threats were received.

The other figure who often accompanied him was Towler, distinctive for his taste in three-piece tweed suits. Today, though, Towler was dressed plainly in a jacket, no tie and checked shirt.

The office of the most influential person in British politics since Margaret Thatcher – arguably since the war – was a small, functional corner room with bare walls, and a window overlooking the roofs and chimney pots of Westminster. On his computer, the screensaver showed a split-screen picture:

on the left, Farage, grinning away in a flat cap; on the right, Michael Caine at his mid-'60s peak.

The 1960s, and the Second World War, are Farage's dream time: his open-top, double-decker battle bus toured the country during the referendum to the tune of the 1963 war film *The Great Escape*. Farage was born in 1964. The 1960s was also the last decade before Britain joined the EEC in 1973.

Leading off Farage's office there was a small smoking terrace – a strip of concrete flagstones, with four garden chairs made of black and white gauze. It was hardly lavish – and you couldn't say anyone got rich from UKIP's Brexit campaign. Halfway through the campaign, in fact, Gawain Towler took a 50 per cent pay cut to double the UKIP press team and take on a deputy. After the vote, he put his house on the market to avoid bankruptcy.

As I interviewed Farage, he smoked away, as did Towler. An open pack of Marlboro Lights sat on the table on the smoking terrace, a green lighter resting on a neighbouring chair.

I had met Farage several years before, on the set of *Newsnight* in BBC Broadcasting House. We had been doing separate items at the end of the show, and both happened to walk out of the studio at the same time, as the programme finished at 11.20 p.m.

'Fancy a drink?' Farage said, gesturing towards the green room, with its well-stocked fridge. You're very welcome to have a drink afterwards at the BBC – it's just that, in these fitness-obsessed, detoxified times, no one ever does.

'Afraid I've got to head home,' I said, in my own fitness-obsessed, detoxified way.

When I told a friend how struck I was by the open friendliness of the offer, my friend said, 'He's not being friendly. He's being an alcoholic.'

I'm not sure he's right. I quite see why lots of people loathe Farage but, for what it's worth, compared to most politicians, he's surprisingly friendly. He never looks over your shoulder for the better offer, talks down to you or ignores you because you have no political worth.

For someone who drinks heavily, he looked surprisingly fit and dapper: slightly tanned, a little shorter than you might expect, immaculately turned out in a powder-blue suit, a multi-coloured, dotted tie, full brogues in black leather and bright red socks. His face, with his protruding, duck-like lips, bears more than a passing resemblance to Moe, the barman in *The Simpsons*.

One attractive female journalist on a political magazine, in her thirties, tells me:

> You can tell he's a ladies' man. I asked him, 'What are you going to do, now that you've won?' He said, 'Take a few girls out to lunch.' He'd never be a groper, like lots of politicians – he's too much of a gentleman for that.

Farage is fond of military and sporting metaphors, like a jolly character out of P. G. Wodehouse. I asked him whether he wrote his speeches.

'I did once get a speechwriter – all those teleprompters and everything,' he said.

> They don't work. I don't write anything down. I like feeling a little bit nervous before a speech. You'll find me just before, saying, 'Why do I do this? I must be mad?' It's a bit like cricket. I imagine you've played a bit of cricket yourself, haven't you? Well, if you're facing a fast bowler, it's probably better if you're a little on edge, if not actually scared.

He punctuates his conversation with jokes, breaking into bouts of wheezing, nicotine-coated laughter. He smokes almost constantly. At one moment, he leapt up mid-interview, saying, 'Excuse me. Must get my cigarettes.'

Still, he bears no obvious sign of being the heavy drinker that is so much part of his public persona. The eyes and suntanned skin are clear; there is no beer belly; no hungover tetchiness or need for a drink during our interview, which lasts from 12.30 p.m. till 1.45 p.m. – peak time for first drink of the day among traditional alcoholics.

I wouldn't be surprised if he drinks a lot less than he likes to let on: not just because no heavy drinker could survive his working hours, but also because, as Winston Churchill knew with the rumours of his epic drinking, he realises a drinker's reputation boosts his appeal as an everyman – holding up the saloon bar, rather than jockeying for position on the sparkling water and the dawn jogs.

He often drinks for the cameras, and makes an effort to

drink with journalists. In the BBC political reporter Ben Wright's 2016 book *Order, Order! The Rise and Fall of Political Drinking*, Farage confided that his upper limit before an interview is five pints.

In his 'Lunch with the *FT*' interview in April 2016 – a sushi and Perrier affair for most interviewees – Farage sank three pints of ale, half a bottle of Château de Lugagnac and a large glass of port.

When I interviewed him at lunchtime, I had cleared my afternoon, in case a heavy drinking session materialised. Rather disappointingly, Farage talked solidly, without a break for lunch or a drink, before his next appointment. All he needed was a regular, mighty drag from his beloved fags.

What he did do was tell lots of stories that involved him drinking heavily.

'Two lads from Sunderland in the John Betjeman in St Pancras yesterday,' he told me at one point. 'Boof, pint of beer, there you go, Nige.'

This fits with a story told by Peter York – the author and co-inventor of the Sloane Ranger. During the referendum campaign, York was sitting next to Farage at lunch at the Adam House club off the Strand in London.

'We had a mixed grill – ideal lunch for Farage, you'd have thought,' says York. 'But I noticed he picked at his sausages and cut the fat off his bacon.

'I had two and a half glasses of the kitchen red on offer and saw he didn't touch a drop throughout lunch.'

At one moment, Farage excused himself for a cigarette.

York joined him, only to see him walk up the road, not to have a smoke, but to make a phone call. They then went back inside the club, where Farage was asked up on stage to give a speech.

'Immediately he picked up the full, untouched wine glass and took it up on stage with him,' says York. 'Once he was on stage, glug, glug, glug…'

There's something unintentionally old-fashioned about Farage – not just the flat caps and the tweed jackets, but the Leslie Phillips lingo – 'fizz' for 'champagne', calling me 'dear boy'. He even mints his own slang: I was lost when he referred to losing 'the big M' – as in momentum – in the referendum campaign.

Like Douglas Carswell, he is fond of military metaphors – referring to UKIP's 'volunteer army'. He says of the Vote Leave leaders, 'You would not want these boys in the trench with Jerry 100 yards away. They'd be back at the château drinking port.

'I knew from June 2015 that this had to be shotgun, not rifle,' he said of the campaign, referring to the spray action of pellets from a shotgun, rather than the single bullet of the rifle. 'We had to reach as far and wide as we possibly could.'

At fifty-two, he seems much older than he actually is – not in looks, but in general demeanour. My contemporaries from Dulwich College, his old school, are only seven years younger but they are utterly different – more urban, with classless accents and clothes.

There's a sort of cheeky chappy, Max Miller side to him, in the way he interposes his serious political chat with well-honed one-liners: 'I always knew they were Lib Dems [on the campaign trail] because I'd go over and say, "Good morning", and they'd be abusive.'

In that sense, he is like Boris Johnson, who is also longing to amuse and, if he sees a joke hoving into view, can't resist grabbing it. Like Farage, Johnson knows the British public essentially find politics boring – throw in a joke, and they'll swallow dull, and sometimes shocking, material with a smile on their face. A spoonful of sugar makes the medicine go down.

The Farage badinage never seems forced or put on – more like he has been transported straight from a 1950s Ealing comedy, mannerisms intact.

Usually, when you meet politicians in the flesh, they are different from their public persona: sometimes deflated, sometimes relaxed, sometimes ruder. Farage is as he comes across on telly – like a comedian, who's always on.

He also talks to you – as Queen Victoria said of Gladstone – as though you were a public meeting. One of his regular tropes is to ask himself literally rhetorical questions, and then answer them himself: 'Do we need some kind of Europe, a co-operative structure where neighbours live and trade together? The answer to that is yes. That might be my next project.'

His advisers interject as he speaks, and he politely lets them do so, with a few encouraging noises. But they speak as if trying to get a word in edgeways, knowing they are mere understudies to the main act.

'I'm perfectly happy if people disagree with me,' he says, talking about the advice given to him by Chris Bruni-Lowe, his campaign director. Like most modern politicians, Farage, for all his independence, closely follows polling and focus groups (in his case, done by Bruni-Lowe).

Farage's manner is bouncy, confident, underlined with a series of jokes he deploys against himself the moment he's in danger of showing off: 'We got 5.8 million people voting UKIP in those two years – amazing. I can't believe it. I wouldn't vote for me!'

The UKIP referendum campaign was straightforward and unchanging – because UKIP's aim, to get out of Europe, was straightforward and unchanging.

Farage, like Daniel Hannan, has been an MEP since 1999, and has been charting its developments closely, even when journalists like me were treating the EU as too dull to report on at length.

'Every newspaper reports the EU as foreign news, page 18 of *The Times*,' he says. 'It's completely obvious that the project was in the process of acceleration not deceleration. Ever since 2008, Brussels was in a terrible panic that the crisis was driving people towards a different type of politics and they wanted to finish the project before anybody objected.'

All Farage wanted was the chance to have a referendum, and that chance came on 23 January 2013, with David Cameron's Bloomberg speech, promising a referendum if the Tories won a majority at the next general election.

'Bloomberg was a tremendous victory for us,' Farage says.

'It was so obvious to me at the time of Bloomberg that any argument that I should have worked from within the Conservative Party to reform things would never have worked – and actually the UKIP tactic of fighting and taking votes from the outside had worked.'

The Cameron strategy was aimed, too, at getting UKIP voters to vote for him at the general election – a strategy which largely worked.

'Post-Bloomberg, everybody from your community [the press] thought the UKIP fox had been shot,' says Farage. 'I mean, this fox has been shot so many times, it must be a rare species.

'Bloomberg validated us. Suddenly, what I was saying was mainstream. It wasn't quite so kooky, wasn't quite the elements of the fruitcakes, was it?'

In fact, it turned out that the next two years marked the high point of UKIP's electoral power.

The first real sign of UKIP's emerging clout was the Eastleigh by-election, held in February 2013, after the resignation of Chris Huhne, who went to jail for getting his wife to take his speeding points. The Liberal Democrats held the seat, but UKIP's vote went up from 1,933 in 2010 to 11,571.

'Why could the polls not predict how we'd do in the Eastleigh by-election?' says Farage.

Because they didn't read there were several thousand people who'd never voted in their lives.

So the next big job for us were the European elections

– which I would say were our dress rehearsal in many ways for the referendum. It was on this issue. It wasn't about anything else. Fighting a big European election campaign was important. And we won. We endured unbelievable abuse in getting there.

At the European elections of 22 May 2014, UKIP won twenty-four seats, an eleven-seat gain; Labour won twenty seats, a seven-seat gain; and the Tories won nineteen seats, a seven-seat loss. The big losers were the Lib Dems, who won only one seat, a ten-seat loss.

'The European elections were a warm-up in terms of the image, the style of campaign,' says Nigel Farage. 'We didn't do a lot different in the referendum.'

In the extraordinary chain of events that led to the result of the European referendum, the European elections were crucial. They buttressed the Tories' fear of losing the general election, courtesy of UKIP voters; they accelerated the Conservative determination to legislate for a referendum. Those same Tories who voted UKIP in the European elections swung back to the Tories for the 2015 general election – but they'd got used to voting flexibly. They largely voted no in the referendum.

And the moderate success of Ed Miliband kept him in his job; if Miliband had been replaced by a more effective leader, the Tories might not have won a general election, and the referendum wouldn't have taken place.

As a result, Farage is pleased that UKIP just failed, by 617 votes, to beat Labour in the Heywood and Middleton

by-election, on 9 October 2014 – in between the Carswell
and Reckless by-election victories.

'We came within a whisker,' he says, 'Of course, thank God
we didn't win because otherwise Miliband would have been
got rid of as leader.'

The really crucial moments for UKIP were that defection
of Douglas Carswell on 28 August 2014, followed by Mark
Reckless on 27 September.

'The Carswell defection was an important moment,' says
Farage.

The Reckless defection was astonishing. The Carswell defection was never going to be a problem because, on the
socio-economics, Clacton is the most Eurosceptic seat by a
mile and, even though Carswell was the MP there, UKIP was
on the march in a very big way.

Rochester was different. Because it was seat number 254
on the socio-economics, it never had the underprivileged
profile that benefited UKIP prospects. It might go UKIP in a
by-election; never in a general election.

What Mark did was stunningly brave. It was a bit like vol-
unteering for a mission you're unlikely to come back from.
The high point of UKIP ever was the Rochester by-election,
where the Tory Party had clearly broken the law at will, spent
unbelievable sums of money, push-polled.

'Push-polling' is when pollsters ring up and attempt to influence your vote while they're talking to you. UKIP claims

Tory push-pollers called, asking voters, 'How do you feel that your MPs are drunk?' They were referring to a moment in July 2010 when Reckless failed to vote in the Commons because he was too drunk.

'It's disgusting what they did,' says Farage.

The two defections took UKIP to new heights.

'We were on a bit of a crest of a wave,' says Farage. 'The Tories had money but we had people.'

Farage was completely aware that Carswell and Reckless had defected in order to push for a referendum, not out of any deep-seated affection for UKIP.

'That's why both of them did it – they did it just to lump that pressure on,' says Farage.

At this stage, though, the aims of the Tate Britain Group and Farage were as one.

After UKIP's two by-election victories and the victory in the European elections, few commentators thought the Conservatives would win a general election or, if they did, that the Brexiteers would win the referendum. But, once Cameron called the referendum in February 2016, the polls went up and down, sometimes predicting Brexit, sometimes not. All the time, UKIP continued to be treated by many as fruitcakes.

'What was interesting was the extraordinary misconception from the commentariat which – still in 2015 – was that UKIP voters were all middle class, half-colonels living in Wiltshire,' says Farage.

In the general election, the Cameron strategy worked.

By promising a referendum, he successfully got voters who had backed UKIP the year before in the European elections to vote Tory in the general election. In the 2014 European elections, UKIP got 4,376,635 votes, and the Tories 3,792,549. In the 2015 general election, the Tories won 11,334,576 votes, UKIP 3,881,099.

'You could argue that it was our votes that got David Cameron his majority,' Farage says. 'William Cash in North Warwickshire – the number two Labour target seat and the Tories win it comfortably.'

Cash, son of the veteran Eurosceptic MP, Sir Bill Cash, polled 8,256 votes for UKIP. The Tories benefited from a 2.1 per cent swing, with 20,042 votes, while Labour slumped by 4 per cent to 17,069. UKIP, with a 14.6 per cent swing, took their votes largely from Labour and the Lib Dems.

'Two million of our Euro election voters voted Tory and we still got four million votes,' says Farage.

But, while UKIP dropped Tory votes, they gained Labour ones.

'The night of the general election, the first result in was Sunderland – funny that Sunderland keeps coming up in our political discourse,' says Farage, referring to the Sunderland result in the referendum, the first significant sign that Brexit had won. Sunderland voted 61 per cent to 39 per cent to leave. In the general election, Labour held Sunderland but UKIP increased their vote by 16.5 per cent.

I was on the telly and I said I wish the editors of the *Mail* and

The Sun had seen this result – and seen what UKIP's done to the Labour vote in Sunderland. And still nobody understood it; nobody believed it. We'd got trapped, in British politics, in this mentality that Euroscepticism was a centre-right thing. Well, of course, historically, it had always been a centre-left thing, or it had been stronger on the centre left.

UKIP also engaged with non-voters.

'Not only did the commentariat miss the fact that we were picking up Labour voters,' says Nigel Farage, 'they missed that lots of our voters in all forms of election – between one in four and one in five – were non-voters.'

During their general election campaign, UKIP polled better on immigration than any other party.

'We decided to make it about immigration in February 2015,' says Chris Bruni-Lowe,

> but Carswell would write articles, saying immigration was positive. He wanted billboards saying 'Positive Immigration'. It was just mad.
>
> I said, 'We've got to do a campaign based on immigration.' I was there when Nigel called Douglas into his office, saying, 'Don't contradict me on this issue of immigration. You don't understand it.' Nigel was right. Immigration was the only thing that got us near 4 million votes.

The battle between Farage and Carswell was kicking off. And it had an odd, highly important result – it meant that Farage decided to renege on his resignation after the 2015 election, and lead the referendum campaign for UKIP.

'In May 2015, there is a huge battle between Carswell and Suzanne Evans [the former UKIP spokesman] to get rid of Farage: to get a different leader, but also they didn't want Nigel to lead the referendum campaign,' says Chris Bruni-Lowe.

On 8 May, the day after the general election, Farage resigned. Shortly afterwards, he rang Bruni-Lowe.

'He said, "You'll never guess what Carswell's just done,"' says Bruni-Lowe.

> He asked Nigel whether or not he wanted to come back as leader in some form. And Nigel said, 'Well, I don't know; maybe with Brexit, I might do.' Carswell said, 'You must not come back, you're toxic, you'll damage the referendum campaign, you'll lose it.' Nigel went, 'Fuck this, I'm staying.' If Carswell had played this right, Farage may have just walked off.

So Farage resumed the leadership of UKIP three days after his resignation, to the relief of many, if not all, UKIP supporters.

The tectonic plates of British politics had lurched. Some psephologists spotted it. But no pundits pointed confidently to the result of an utterly changed political landscape – a vote for Brexit, little over a year after the general election, and the mass clear-out of Nos 10 and 11 Downing Street.

CHAPTER 3

VOTE LEAVE:
THE SOUTH BANK SHOW

After the general election victory in May 2015, the Tate Britain Group were confident the strategy was working. Carswell and Reckless had defected; Cameron had made his Bloomberg speech.

They had the promise of a referendum in the bag and it looked like the Farage Paradox was being successfully squashed.

'UKIP's doing well in the polls and there's been no discernible increase in support for Remain – that's most important,' says Carswell.

Now the crucial thing for some Leavers was to sort out a Brexit campaign that continued to crush the Farage Paradox.

'Everyone could see that if the Out campaign was run as Leave.EU [the campaign supported by Nigel Farage] wanted it to be run, it would be a disaster,' says Carswell.

Enter Matthew Elliott, the chief executive of Vote Leave.

Elliott, thirty-eight, has a deceptively diffident air, with a hesitant speaking manner, punctuated by nervous laughter. He seems an unlikely figure to pull off two political campaign victories, first in the 2011 Alternative Vote referendum, and then in the EU referendum.

It was Elliott's victory in 2011, preventing the introduction of the Alternative Vote at general elections, that persuaded Daniel Hannan to appoint him as chief executive of Vote Leave. Elliott had begun his Eurosceptic career early – his first job after leaving LSE was working for Sir Bill Cash, the veteran Eurosceptic MP.

Elliott's strategy in 2011 had been simple – to concentrate on the expense of installing electronic voting machines for the AV vote. Posters were put up of a baby in hospital, saying, 'She needs a new maternity facility not an alternative vote system. Say NO to spending £250m on AV. Our country can't afford it. NO to AV.'

The same line was used of military flak jackets – better to spend money on them than on AV.

'I thought it was a rubbish argument at first, but the more I watched him, the more I realised how clever he was being,' says Daniel Hannan. 'I made a note then and there to approach him when we eventually got our In/Out vote.'

The same money-saving message would be echoed in the European referendum, in Vote Leave's emphasis on the £350 million a week Britain spends on the EU. During the referendum, there was an almighty row over that figure being gross, rather than net. In the AV campaign, there were similar criticisms that the supposed £250 million figure included money spent on the referendum itself; that the system wouldn't cost as much as that.

Whatever the truth of the matter, the pro-Alternative Vote campaign didn't cut through – and Elliott was in the ascendant.

What became Vote Leave was planned ten days after the general election of 7 May 2015. Matthew Elliott, Bernard Jenkin and Steve Baker (the latter both MPs) and the spread-betting tycoon Stuart Wheeler consulted both Dominic Cummings and Daniel Hannan.

A group, formed of Elliott, Jenkin, Owen Paterson and Steve Baker, were sounding out donors, trying to set up the group to win the referendum. Cummings helped plan how to sort out the government structure, the donors, how to deal with UKIP and MPs.

This continued from mid-May to the end of July, with meetings taking place in the office of the Conservative MP Owen Paterson – popularly referred to by some of the Leavers as O-Pattz, following in the footsteps of R-Pattz, the nickname of hot young actor Robert Pattinson.

In 2013, Elliott had set up Business for Britain, fighting for a reformed Europe. On this skeleton, Vote Leave was built. Within six weeks of Vote Leave's foundation, money was coming in from Wheeler and others. From the beginning, cracks emerged, which would widen into a full-scale coup six months down the line.

A colleague of Dominic Cummings says, 'Dom's view was that Elliott is useless and working with him would be awful but Dom thought he could co-opt him and corral him further on down the line, which is what he did.'

Vote Leave's lack of activity had been noted by Nigel Farage and his principal backer, Arron Banks, an insurance tycoon. Until 13 April 2016 – when Vote Leave got official designation by the Electoral Commission, and the right to spend £7 million on the campaign – the real war was between Vote Leave and Leave.EU, founded by Banks.

UKIP had been planning its referendum campaign in earnest immediately after the general election. In June 2015, Chris Bruni-Lowe did a big, 10,000-strong poll, for Farage and Banks.

'The one big difference in the referendum to anything we've ever done before is we were miles ahead of the press,' says Farage. 'Last June, we spent a lot of money in the days after the general election.'

Bruni-Lowe put immigration – particularly Turkish accession to the EU and Angela Merkel's Syrian measures – to Farage as his number one item on the agenda in June 2015.

'He was quite right,' says Farage.

You can't argue with facts. I find that, after a while working with an adviser, you start thinking the same things.

We knew that issues like Turkey, open-door immigration, what Merkel had done, were crucial. Of course, the sovereignty stuff was very important. Of course, there are niche arguments about the fishing industry. If you want to win, there's got to be a big message to a big audience. We knew it was immigration.

I always said to people that immigration is a subset of governing your own country. It's a reason that the slogan that I chose for the campaign was 'We want our country back'. Assertive, strong, clear and actually positive. And the symbolism I used was the passport, being the emblematic symbol of what had gone wrong in my view. It summed it up a dream.

Farage then concentrated on immigration and Turkish admission into the EU in public meetings across the country.

'We took this data to Vote Leave in June 2015, and they said, "No, it's not an issue. It turns off undecideds." I showed them – for 3,000 undecideds, it was their number one issue.'

Because Nigel Farage as an individual has more political reach than UKIP as a whole, the UKIP team also decided to separate the two for the campaign.

'There's nothing with UKIP and Nigel for months in the campaign,' says Chris Bruni-Lowe. 'At roadshows, there were no UKIP logos. There was, "Just come and see Nigel Farage."'

In June 2015, the Midlands Industrial Council did a cruise around the Channel Islands. Farage and Bruni-Lowe were aboard, as were several major Leave donors, and Matthew Elliott, later to be head of the Vote Leave campaign.

'On the boat, Elliott was going to give his vision,' says Chris Bruni-Lowe. 'But Elliott isn't fundamentally very good. He has the turning circle of the *QE2*. He doesn't really get it.'

By this stage, the Remain side had already got their operation into gear. Britain Stronger in Europe was officially launched on 12 October 2015, and became the official Remain campaign in April 2016. Unlike the Leave operation, there was no internal fighting between various Remain factions to become the top dog.

'They've already got a head start on us,' says Bruni-Lowe.

On the cruise, I said to Elliott, 'We're still Business for Britain [a sort of precursor of Vote Leave], we're still undecided.' A lot of donors behind Business for Britain were reformers; they didn't want to leave. The list of Out businesses is crappy – the business chamber of commerce in Bradford is perfectly fine; but it's not your business heavyweights.

The embryonic Leave campaigns were also short of funds in the summer of 2015.

'We needed money – we'd already been geeing up Arron Banks,' says Bruni-Lowe.

Nigel said he wanted to play a role. What is that role? [The Vote Leave contingent] don't know. Nigel's view was that he didn't want to be the person of the campaign – his view was that Kate Hoey should run the campaign. He wanted to be one of them. When we were on the cruise, he said, 'Let's get everyone round the table, and sort out what different jobs people will do, jobs for Nigel, Bill Cash, Eurosceptic businessmen. But Matthew's problem is, he quite likes running stuff himself.

To outsider journalists like me, it all looked very chaotic – and it was. In fact, though, the inactivity of Vote Leave in the summer of 2015 was rather helpful for the Leave side – it galvanised Leave.EU into action, which in turn kicked Vote Leave into gear.

'Arron Banks turns up and says, "You and all these MPs don't know anything," says Dominic Cummings. "'You need someone like me to run the Out campaign. I'm going to do it with Nigel." That was useful because it pushed Elliott. Suddenly there are these rivals around.'

In July 2015, the Cummings–Elliott group agreed on developing a new organisation. At that time, they were planning a response to what would be a yes or no question in the referendum.

'That would have been much easier,' says Cummings. 'We could have used all the material Maurice Saatchi had developed for the No to the Euro campaign.'

That campaign, which ran from 2000 to 2004, when Gordon Brown ruled out joining the euro, was simply called the 'No Campaign'.

'It was going to be just the No Campaign – a complete copy,' says Dominic Cummings. 'That got kiboshed because Cameron changed the question to Leave or Remain. It was quite wise. "Leave" is stark.'

Cummings began to corral a small, cross-party group of MPs and MEPs to form the parliamentary wing of Vote Leave: Bernard Jenkin, Steve Baker, Kate Hoey, Graham Stringer, Douglas Carswell, Daniel Hannan, Owen Paterson. This exploratory committee would coalesce with Business for Britain to form the Vote Leave campaign.

Cummings started biking round London, recruiting employees and raising money.

By August, it was all agreed. Elliott, the cross-party group of MPs and the donors were all on board. A new legal structure was set up. They found an office in Westminster Tower on Albert Embankment, on the south bank of the Thames. They moved into their HQ in September and started using the big, main room, with a few meeting rooms leading off it, even as it was being renovated. The office wasn't finished until the end of December.

From the beginning, Cummings had worked out the three pillars of the campaign that remained till the end: take back control; cost; and safe option. In other words, staying in isn't the safer option: because the status quo doesn't exist, because the EU keeps changing, the safer option was to take back control and leave the EU.

'[The three pillars] were written on the wall of the office from the beginning,' says Victoria Woodcock, Vote Leave's director of operations. 'Dom wrote them on the wall in marker pen, which would have to be painted over before we could let the building go.'

Matthew Elliott and Dominic Cummings framed the campaign immediately as a non-party political – particularly a non-UKIP political – one.

'If it wasn't a campaign where people like Gisela Stuart and Priti Patel and Frank Field were totally comfortable, it was lost,' says Douglas Carswell. 'We saw this and we saw it a long way off, and we did something about it.'

Figures at UKIP and Leave.EU were still concerned by the apparent lack of direction at Vote Leave.

'Cummings's aim was to work in Downing Street for Gove,' says Chris Bruni-Lowe. 'He was also still pushing the idea of two referendums. It was a Conservative and self-interested campaign.'

Cummings denies he was planning then to work in Downing Street for Gove – or, as Farage suggested, for Cameron.

'Farage started saying to me, "You guys aren't going to do anything. What you really want is jobs with Cameron,"' says Cummings, who has been outspoken in his criticism of David Cameron, calling him 'a sphinx without a riddle'.

> I said, 'Nigel, people say a lot of awful things about me. But one thing you can't say is that I want a job with David Cameron. Very few people have been publicly ruder about him than me. The idea that I'm doing this to get a job with him is silly.'

The other suggestion is that Cummings was already positioning himself as chief of staff in a future Gove administration.

'Why would I do the Out campaign if I wanted to work with Michael in Downing Street?' says Cummings. 'We're friends anyway. Why make my life hell for a year?'

Cummings had previously got on well with Farage but, around the time of the general election, something happened.

'In March 2015, I'd seen him and he was very friendly and sensible and reasonably sane about the referendum,' says Cummings. 'He asked me about his role in the referendum.

I said, "You've got a role in it but you can't run it. It can't be seen as the Nigel Farage show." He said, "I agree."'

'Farage changed enormously,' continues Cummings.

> I'd probably talked to him half a dozen times before. I was genuinely quite surprised when he said, 'I know what you're up to. You're not here for a cause – you're here for Downing Street.'
>
> I said to him, 'You and I have sat in Stuart Wheeler's castle quite a few times in the last ten years. You know me.' He changed.

Daniel Hannan also noticed a sea change in Nigel Farage at around the same time.

'Nigel's whole personality changed,' says Hannan. 'Everyone in UKIP noticed it. Even his closest supporters were shaken by how sudden the transformation was. One of them told me that every single MEP recognised [UKIP MEP] Patrick O'Flynn's description of him as having almost overnight become "snarling and thin-skinned".'

By June 2015, Farage was taking on a very different manner with Cummings.

'It was all about the debates – who's going to be in them,' says Cummings.

> I said, 'Nigel, the people who lead the debates should be the ones that empirical research says the public trusts most. If that's you, that's you. If it isn't, it isn't. Winning is the important thing. You of all people should accept that.'

Farage said, 'The research is already clear – I'm trusted. I'm the person who should lead the debate.' My heart sank after that.

A crucial element in the build-up to the referendum was what individuals thought the result would be. According to Dominic Cummings, Nigel Farage 'definitely thought we're obviously going to lose. He always thought that, he said that.'

Then, if UKIP were faced with losing the referendum – and their central goal of leaving the EU was scotched – they, and Nigel Farage, had to find other ways of justifying their careers.

'Farage said, "One of the goals is getting out of the EU,"' says Dominic Cummings. 'He thinks UKIP has a role in general.' In other words, a political purpose that had nothing to do with getting out of the EU.

Another factor was that UKIP was short of money – a problem solved if they got official designation and access to the £7 million of referendum funding that came with it.

Whatever the truth of these increasingly fractious shenanigans between Vote Leave and UKIP, Vote Leave still seemed alarmingly inactive to UKIP in the summer of 2015.

Frustrated by this apparent lack of urgency, Bruni-Lowe decided to ginger things up at the UKIP conference in September.

'There's nothing going on – why don't we back Arron Banks, as a way of causing a complete stir with Vote Leave, to make everyone go head to head?' says Bruni-Lowe.

We spent six months terrorising Elliott. They wanted to win this debate as if they were at the Oxford Union, on a high level. We wanted to get down on a normal level.

In September, Nigel and I said we've got to kick Elliott off the fence or we'll lose.

Bruni-Lowe did so by leaking a story to the *Daily Express*, saying that Arron Banks was putting £20 million into a campaign other than Vote Leave, in order 'to make it competitive'.

In October 2015, Vote Leave was launched, with its new name chosen to deal with the Leave/Remain question now confirmed on the ballot paper.

'Elliott launched in a rush,' says Chris Bruni-Lowe. 'The website was rubbish. They were briefing against Nigel, too: "He's toxic, he wants to lose."'

By this point, Dominic Cummings had also formulated the main campaign messages.

'I'd already spent a lot of time over the previous ten to fifteen years, thinking about what people think and don't think,' he says. 'Before the election, I'd been doing focus groups for people, and I'd throw Europe stuff into the mix. The most effective slogan was "Keep the Pound, Keep Control" on the euro campaign. You couldn't beat that theme.'

Indeed, it would emerge as the principal slogan of the Vote Leave campaign. It began as 'Take control' before being slightly altered to 'Take back control'. It was decided, too, that 'Vote Leave' sounded better – a more direct call to the ballot box – than just 'Leave'.

'Control, take back control, was in my mind,' says
Cummings.

A combination of that plus the money spent on the EU, plus
the NHS. I started the polling, focus groups, different data,
looking at the numbers, trying to balance it all out.

 You look for the big things, where there are 30 per cent
gaps [between approval and disapproval ratings], telling you
fundamental things. There was a massive gap on core things
like take back control, controlled immigration, that we could
spend our money better on the NHS.

It was the tussling over these issues – particularly immigration – that was to cause such trouble over the next nine
months, leading up to the referendum. To put it simply,
Nigel Farage wanted immigration front and centre in the
campaign; Dominic Cummings didn't.

'Take back control and immigration are connected,' says
Cummings.

You don't have to say immigration [explicitly, in the Vote Leave
campaign]. At a very deep level, if people weren't bothered by
immigration, we wouldn't have stood a chance. It's also the
case that, by the time of the referendum, immigration was
such a concern you didn't have to explain it; you just had to
ask people whether they thought it's safer to take back control.

 It's not like a normal political issue, which is very hard to
get across to the public. The immigration debate is completely

different. The public already knew everything about it, and they knew what they thought about it.

You had a backdrop of boats coming over, people drowning, carnage.

With news of the European migration crisis dominating the headlines, much of Vote Leave's work on immigration was being done by the media. That was particularly handy when the group was short of money. Even when they got designation as the official Leave campaign, that only entitled them to £7 million – not very much in the grand scheme of things.

'You're in a country where you can't buy TV ads, you can't spend a billion dollars, you cannot buy that kind of communication,' says Cummings. 'The fundamentals are already outside of our control or David Cameron's control. If Cameron gets a deal – free movement is ended in the following ways – that might change the debate.'

In fact, the general political climate in Britain and Europe helped the Vote Leave campaign. 'People have had more than a decade post-9/11 of crazy Muslims slipping through the immigration net,' Cummings says. 'Seven million pounds in relation to that is nothing. Farage was saying we've got to spend it on immigration. I was saying, "It's nothing."'

Cummings determined that immigration was already on the minds of Leave voters and potential Leave voters.

'The point is what we as a campaign say about it,' he says. 'This is a huge, massive thing dominating psychology. We should spend our media time on what people don't know about it. Everyone knows immigration is out of control; that the EU plays a major part in that. They don't know how much money is spent on it.'

That's why, from September 2015, Vote Leave devoted its time to questions about money, the NHS and taking back control. It was then that the famous £350 million figure was deployed – the amount of money spent each week by Britain on the EU – and it was connected to NHS spending.

'Everyone cares about the NHS but they don't think about it in the context of the EU,' says Cummings. 'You have to get people thinking of something other than immigration. If they think it's just immigration, some of them are going to vote for us, but a lot of other people aren't. With the NHS, the £350 million, you get them thinking about other things.'

A big row simmered through the campaign over that £350 million figure, emblazoned across Vote Leave buses. It was the gross contribution Britain made to the EU; in fact, Britain got half that figure back, meaning the net spend was £175 million a week.

'[The £350 million] was a disastrous mistake,' says Farage.

What our polling showed us in June 2015, when you asked the British people what EU membership costs, most thought a million pounds a day – hardly anyone thought it was more than £10 million a day.

It didn't matter what the figure was. It just had to be one that was bombproof. If you'd said £50 million for a week for the NHS, it would have had just as big an impact. It's irrelevant. It's telephone numbers. I begged Gove to get rid of it. But he wouldn't do it.

I just knew that, in the aftermath, if we won, they'd never let us forget it. That was a mistake.

Like so much of the Leave campaign, the various sides have fundamental differences of opinion over it – and it's impossible to say definitively what worked and what didn't work.

Still, even Douglas Carswell, the pro-immigration UKIP MP, approved of the £350 million line.

'The £350 million gross contribution is a fact,' Carswell says.

And, if you're going to go around saying £350 million a week is not a lot of money, thanks for highlighting how out of touch you are in the country.

I stand by that figure. Among the voters who mattered, they got it. If you were paid an amount of money, you wouldn't state your salary as a net figure; you'd use the gross figure.

If we'd used the net figure, Remain broadcasters still wouldn't have said that's fair. They sounded like Romanovs quibbling about their Fabergé eggs: if you're a swing voter in Clacton, and the maternity unit is threatened with closure, if you hear someone saying £350 million is a small amount and, besides, it's only £175 million…

Cummings, too, realised that it was an instantly understandable thing.

'If you say, what do you think of some general idea of freedom, they don't know what you're talking about,' says Cummings.

> If you say, 'We spend £350 million a week, which we could spend on the NHS,' they're outraged. Even if you say the other side say it's a lie, they think, 'Maybe they are lying, but we're definitely spending more money than we get back, and that's better spent on the NHS.'
>
> The gross–net row gets people thinking – the core truth is we're net contributors to the EU budget. It's a massive amount of money – even half of it – and we could spend it better.

These reactions were gauged by Cummings, using a series of focus groups – much the most popular way these days for experts to harvest public opinion. Everyone uses them, from the giant market research agency ICM to Sir Lynton Crosby, who delivered election victory for the Tories in 2015 and two mayoral victories for Boris Johnson.

Each focus group usually consists of eight people selected from a particular socio-economic background. They don't come cheap – costing from £1,000 to £8,000 for each group. The most important element is the right recruiter: the person on the ground who can recruit eight people who come as close as possible to genuinely reflecting a particular type of person. Vote Leave did a lot of focus groups and did them all over the country.

'You get a lot of good ideas from them,' says Dominic Cummings. 'You refine it, you change the language, you massively simplify things. MPs are all interested in 1,000 things. But ordinary people strip out 90 per cent of data, and they're left with this – we're net contributors and we could spend the money better.'

Cummings's other great data-harvesting device took the form of three physicists he had recruited.

'The great moment was when Dom discovered the computer scientists who had learnt how to strip information from Facebook about potential voters,' says Daniel Hannan. 'At a low cost, we had a brilliant way of targeting our campaign.'

As soon as Cummings took the job at Vote Leave, he recruited his three physicists, experts in computation, physics and data science. When Cummings hired them, they'd never done anything in politics before.

The physicists first researched global literature on what has been shown with good evidence to work – and not work – in political campaigning. They then built models to try to predict who would be on the Leave side. They used demographics, conventional polls and new ideas about polls. These models were then all adjusted with data taken from the real world – both physical (i.e. leaflets and canvassing) and online, Facebook in particular.

'They were extremely clever, far cleverer than anyone else [on the campaign],' says Cummings.

Modern elections are data wars: both sides gather as much information as possible on voters, and target them to evoke their sympathies and bring out the vote. You can now buy commercial databases for millions of pounds.

'Data is often talked about by people in politics,' says Douglas Carswell.

> Very few people understand it and Dominic is one of them. The traditional idea is you've got broadcast media and press media, and social media as a poor cousin. That's completely changed. Dom has understood this better than anyone else in the world.
>
> Many people misunderstand Facebook. They think it's a question of likes. They're largely irrelevant. It's what people do with it, whether they engage with it, pass it on. There was this extraordinary amount of activity – a firestorm going on. Many of the pundits on the broadcast media didn't even know about it. It was totally different to the narrative going out on *Newsnight* every night. That's why we won.

From the beginning of the campaign, Cummings knew the polls were skewed.

'All the way along, we were obviously underdogs,' he remembers. 'The physicists said, if the polls are 50–50 on the day, you'll win; even if you're a little behind, you'll win.'

One of the reasons the polls got the referendum wrong was the echo bubble that is London.

'All the pollsters live in London, they'll fudge things in the other direction [because they think] "98 per cent of my friends are voting in," so they think it's going the other way,' says Cummings. 'We know different because we've got empirical evidence the other way.'

Cummings and the physicists had also found a way of extracting the information at a fraction of the price.

The physicists looked at the referendum from a pure data point of view. They found wizardly ways of stripping information out of Facebook and lots of other digital sources for free, and then reconstructed it. Building complex mathematical models, they predicted what sorts of people were likely to vote Leave.

'We found new ways of finding out what people think,' says Cummings.

And, using very large samples of data, that enabled us to break things down into far smaller subgroups than normal. With a normal 1,000-person poll, you can't break that down into, say, women between twenty and thirty who live in Wales, or who went to a Russell Group university. It's impossible – there are no statistics.

By mining the internet, the physicists extracted a huge amount of information about the potential voting population. They also calculated what the key motivations were among various demographics. Just as Facebook breaks up its users into different demographics to target them with tailored adverts, so Vote Leave did the same, and fired off computer-guided ads.

'We ran almost one billion adverts, aimed at all kinds of people,' says Cummings.

As much as 99 per cent of the advertising budget was digital – then you can track and measure the reaction, to see who clicks on what.

You come up with a creative idea. You figure out who to send it to. You send it. You see how many hits there are. A bunch of reactions happen. The data streams out. The physicists collect the data and then go, 'Here's what we've learnt.' You then use that information to change and update your models.

Vote Leave's campaign director also took the physicists along to meetings with the main pollsters, disguising them as interns and webmasters.

'A couple of times, people said to them, "You're the web guy, what's your name?"' says Cummings.

But none of the pollsters actually twigged who the physicists were.

'They had no idea they were talking to a professor of quantum mechanics,' says Cummings. 'The physicists would ask them things like, "How does this work exactly? When you say error, how do you define that?"'

The physicists came away thinking all the polls were flawed, particularly those by Populus. They acknowledged that YouGov's were the most mathematically efficient.

'They met lots of pollsters and said, "This business has huge problems. We can do some innovations that no one's done before,"' says Cummings. And so the physicists then went away and did their own research into voting patterns.

'We had guys who'd worked on the Large Hadron Collider, the biggest data project in the world,' says Cummings. 'They trawled the world and said, "Here are the actual academic papers, with the proper methodology that you can learn real things from."'

Not everyone in the Leave camp was convinced by the planet-brained, digital approach to the referendum.

'There are more effective ways of campaigning than social media and focus groups,' says Sir Bill Cash, the Eurosceptic MP. 'A much better approach is to get out there, to talk to people, to tell them the facts. There's an integrity about that sort of debate. David Davis and I were keen on GO [the Grassroots Out campaign], because they used the grassroots, the activists on the ground.'

It was this difference in approach to campaigning between Dominic Cummings and other Brexiteers that, at the beginning of 2016, led to the failed coup to get rid of Cummings.

CHAPTER 4

A COMEDY OF ERRORS:
THE VERY BRITISH COUP

To the outside world, the Leave operation looked a mess at the beginning of 2016 – a loose-knit group of preening ferrets in a sack, clawing each other to death in the fight for designation as the official campaign.

Vote Leave was low in the water, fighting for its life – largely dependent on the money of Peter Cruddas, the banker and former co-treasurer of the Conservative Party, and Stuart Wheeler.

'It was pretty much hand to mouth,' says Victoria Woodcock, director of operations at Vote Leave. 'Before designation, you can spend as much money as you want to, but we didn't have the cash. Someone described the campaign once as trying to build a jumbo jet as it was taking off.'

'It was a very close-run thing,' agrees Douglas Carswell. 'The thing that was the most frustrating was that we needed to do work far, far out [from the referendum], but we couldn't get the money to do that work because donors kept on saying you need to get your act together.'

As with everything in the byzantine world of the various Leave groups, fighting their Judean People's Front wars, there was an added complication.

Members of the board of Vote Leave – chief among them Bernard Jenkin, the Tory MP – were not happy with the way Dominic Cummings was running the show.

Vote Leave insiders say storm clouds had been gathering since late 2015. Other Leave organisations appeared to be stealing a march on Vote Leave. Remain seemed to be powering ahead.

Some Vote Leave donors felt they weren't getting much bang for their buck. They were aggrieved when they weren't given notice of Vote Leave stunts – like the one played by young activists who infiltrated the Confederation of British Industry's London conference, addressed by David Cameron, on 9 November 2015. The protesters brandished banners, chanting, 'CBI, Voice of Brussels.'

The stunt was synchronised to take place on the same day Vote Leave wrote a letter to the new CBI director-general, Carolyn Fairbairn. The letter claimed the business lobby was 'more interested in promoting the EU than fighting for what is good for Britain'.

Although some Eurosceptic campaigners didn't like these guerrilla tactics, they were effective. As a result, the CBI became wary of being too openly Europhile. And Europhile businessmen became wary of being the victims of future stunts – no FTSE 100 chairman wants his pinstripe suit to be egged on the way into the AGM.

'[The CBI stunt] did what it was meant to do – it put uncertainty into whether anyone should trust the CBI,' says Victoria Woodcock.

'Me and Victoria Woodcock were running it,' says Dominic Cummings. 'She was officially director of operations but was in fact CEO. She's the single most important member of staff. She ran the whole thing.'

'Under Matthew's name, it just says fund-raising; under Dom, it was the whole campaign,' says Woodcock. 'He [Matthew] was very worried if we did something rash. Without Dom, we wouldn't have won.'

Several Eurosceptic MPs disapproved of the direction of Vote Leave at this time, among them Sir Bill Cash, the Maastricht veteran.

'I was not at all happy with the idea of Dominic Cummings running this operation, from my past awareness of him,' says Sir Bill.

They weren't mentioning immigration or the much-needed grassroots campaign.

And the structure of Vote Leave was inadequate. In August 2015, concerned about operational structure, I did a company search – Elliott and Cummings were the only two directors and shareholders. I was deeply concerned. There were no company solicitors or accountants. I made it clear that they had to have company solicitors. You can't carry on like this. Where is the accountability, the chain of command?

Sir Bill Cash arranged for a firm of solicitors to work for Vote Leave but he remained unconvinced that their advice was being followed.

'It was run on a bunker basis,' says Sir Bill.

> The impression I got was that Cummings ran it. Their web-site was extremely bland. Leave.EU had a very lively website.
>
> On their website, [Vote Leave] had a whole attack on Members of Parliament, without explaining that it was Parliament – through backbench MPs – that had achieved so much from Maastricht onwards. Every EU treaty had been subject to extreme analysis by backbenchers. The whole object of the referendum was to restore democracy to Parliament.

Chris Grayling, the Eurosceptic Cabinet minister – nick-named 'The Graylord' by some Brexiteers – hadn't yet come out for Leave publicly. But he was also instrumental in the anti-Cummings manoeuvres from behind the scenes.

'Matthew Elliott was persuaded to go along with the coup by Chris Grayling,' says Dominic Cummings.

> Grayling was trying to figure out a way to preserve a place in the Cabinet [by ensuring he was suitably prominent in the cam-paign]. He went to Elliott and said, 'I won't support Vote Leave while Cummings is there. You don't want this guy there. He's

going to get all the credit if this thing works out. You should get rid of him and you will be the hero of the whole thing.'

Grayling moved in January. He wanted to shake everything up so he could become chairman of the official campaign.

That January, the Vote Leave donor Stuart Wheeler had a gathering at Chilham Castle in Kent.

'Afterwards, Matthew Elliott rang me up and said, "We've all decided we've got to move Dominic," because he had become an impediment to raising money,' says Bernard Jenkin. 'That is why the board unanimously agreed that Dominic should be moved to an advisory role.'

Different groups in the coup had different motives but they all agreed on one thing – that Cummings had to go.

'Because I wouldn't let them be in charge,' says Cummings.

The plots and alliances became exceedingly complicated. Daniel Hannan didn't want to merge Vote Leave with Arron Banks and Leave.EU. Chris Grayling hoped to become chairman of the merged entity, with Banks as co-chairman and Elliott as CEO – and Cummings on the scrapheap.

Cummings recalls, 'They said they wanted a merger and I said, "Arron Banks and Andy Wigmore [Leave.EU head of communications] aren't fit and proper people to be running a campaign. We are not going to merge with these people. They're clowns."'

According to Cummings, Farage, too, wanted him out of the way in order to arrange a merger of the various Leave groups, ideally with him and Arron Banks running the show.

'For Farage, the crucial thing was the debates – to be the officially nominated entity to debate against David Cameron,' says Cummings.

On top of all this, several members of the Vote Leave board were unhappy with Cummings's strategy. They were particularly exercised by a Vote Leave leaflet emphasising how the NHS could be saved by leaving the EU – a leaflet that appealed to the left more than the right.

'They hated it,' says Victoria Woodcock.

They hated that it hadn't been cleared through them. They always wanted to talk about the technicalities of the EU – [even though] no one will listen to you – no one could understand it. Fundamentally, they didn't agree with Dom – and so wanted to get rid of him.

I later discovered that Bernard Jenkin and Chris Grayling and Matthew Elliott were behind the coup.

All this bubbling anger and all the simmering feuds meant Jenkin led the coup to sack Cummings.

'Bernard and co. thought, rightly, that, if Dominic stays here, he'll run it the way he wants to run it, and me and my friends are marginalised,' says Dominic Cummings.

'The only reason it's called a coup is because that's what Dominic decided to call it,' says Bernard Jenkin. 'When a board, completely united, decides that something needs to be done, and the executive resists it, whose coup is it?'

According to Cummings, the MPs were worried that – if and when Michael Gove joined the Vote Leave campaign – they would be marginalised, and wouldn't be able to get rid of Cummings. 'They thought, "We've got to get rid of the fucker." Which is a rational thought – "Once Gove comes over, we're knackered." And they were. They didn't have any more say in anything.'

And so the coup began. On 26 January 2016, Dominic Cummings was due to have a meeting with a board member of Vote Leave.

'The coup was a comedy of errors,' says Cummings. 'I thought the meeting was in my office. The board member rang up and said, "Where are you?" I said, "I'm waiting." They said the meeting was in Tufton Street.'

Tufton Street is in the shadow of Westminster Abbey, across the Thames from the Vote Leave offices.

'If I'd known there was an official meeting there, I'd have thought there's a rabbit off,' says Cummings. 'But, because it seemed like it was a cock-up, I went there.'

The attempted coup was straight out of the Mafia playbook – although Don Corleone would have arranged it rather more efficiently and ruthlessly.

'What you always try and do is you do it away from the rest of the staff – they might go mad; there might be a scene,' says Cummings.

Cummings walked into the Tufton Street office, sat down and there was Daniel Hodson, a board member and the former chief executive of LIFFE, the futures exchange.

According to Cummings, Hodson said, 'The meeting isn't about what you thought it was going to be about. There's been an agreement that you have to stand down as campaign director. There are some other members of the board here, and a team of lawyers, and a contract to offer to you.'

At this moment, several other directors trooped into the room, among them Bernard Jenkin. The coup plotters then laid out their terms.

'They say, "You've got to go, you say publicly that it's because your wife's pregnant, you'll remain as a consultant, financially you'll be taken care of,"' says Cummings.

At the time of the coup, Dominic Cummings's wife, Mary Wakefield, a columnist at *The Spectator* magazine, was indeed pregnant.

As Cummings recalls the scene: 'I say, "You guys haven't thought this through; you don't know what you're doing. You're not going to have a team because they won't work for Elliott and you guys."'

'One coup plotter said, "He's a complete genius – everyone knows that. He's built this team. You're the problem."'

Cummings said, 'You don't understand what's happened here. These key people are working here because I got them here. These people will not stay and work with you. You guys don't know what you're doing.'

'You're wrong about that,' the plotters said, according to Cummings. 'Anyway, it doesn't matter. You've got to sign this piece of paper.'

They gave Cummings a fifty-page contract, which Cummings suggested he might read elsewhere.

'No – you're not going anywhere to read it,' said one plotter. 'You've got to sign this and you're not leaving this room until it's signed.'

Cummings burst out laughing and said, 'You guys really don't know what you're doing.'

At this moment, Daniel Hannan arrived with Matthew Elliott, the chief executive of Vote Leave, who had been co-opted into the coup.

'Matthew had been bullied into it,' says Cummings. 'They'd called him the previous week, as he later admitted to me.'

Cummings then said to the gathered plotters, 'You guys are being very silly if you think you can force me to stay in the room and sign this.'

He pointed at one plotter and said, 'You know you're making a mistake and you don't even actually mean it, do you?'

This plotter said, 'No. Of course you're free to leave the room. But we would like you to look at this and sign. Our lawyers are waiting outside.'

Behind the glass doors, Cummings could make out the silhouettes of three lawyers pacing around.

He said, 'You've completely fucked this whole process up. You haven't spoken to the key people. You don't know what they're going to do.'

Cummings said he'd leave and go round the corner to the Pret a Manger at the end of Tufton Street to read the contract.

He also suggested some plotters should cross the Thames to the Vote Leave office and talk to the people there.

In fact, what Cummings did was walk round the corner and phone Cleo Watson, the Vote Leave head of outreach, who was in the office.

Cummings said to her:

Cleo, there's a coup. Get Parky [Stephen Parkinson, head of the ground campaign], Vicks [Victoria Woodcock, director of operations] and Paul [Stephenson, director of communications] in a room now, instantly. This is DEFCON 1. These guys have left and they'll be there in two or three minutes. This conversation never happened. There's one chance for this to work out.

Cummings then told Parkinson, Woodcock and Stephenson, over the speakerphone, 'If you three say, "We're going to walk out instantly," they might bottle it.'

They said, 'Got it, right, bye.'

'We knew there was no option – we'd have to walk out,' says Victoria Woodcock. 'There was a sense of loyalty. But also we knew it would have an impact on the media viewpoint. If he did leave, the people who would have been running the campaign would have run us into the ground. We will lose the referendum.'

A minute later, Alan Halsall, co-chairman of Business for Britain and a member of the Vote Leave board, came into the office and, according to Cummings, said to Parkinson,

Woodcock and Stephenson, 'Can I speak to you? Very sorry – it's been agreed that Dominic's going to be a consultant, and Matthew will be in charge of the whole thing.'

Victoria Woodcock said, 'If you do this [get rid of Dom], I will go.'

Parkinson and Stephenson said the same thing.

An argument ensued, which ended with the Cummings loyalists saying, 'Either Dominic stays or we're going now.'

Meanwhile, Cleo Watson went to tell several other workers at Vote Leave what was going on.

'I said, "They're trying to sack Dom,"' says Watson. 'They said, "Oh well, I'm going then."'

Soon after all this, one of the plotting board members called up Cummings and asked him to the Vote Leave office.

'We've got a problem,' said the plotter. 'All the staff are going to walk out if you don't stay. So we need to sort out a new deal.'

'Right. What new deal are you suggesting?' asked Cummings.

'Will you stay?'

'I'll stay if it's agreed that we're in charge; the MPs are not in charge.'

And so it proved. Contrary to the testimony of Cummings, Woodcock and Watson, another source at Vote Leave claims they were always trying to get Cummings to sign a long-term contract that kept him working through to referendum day. Until then, they say, he hadn't contracted to work for the duration.

So the coup came to an end – not that it was the first

one. In November 2015, Bernard Jenkin had already tried to remove Cummings – whose management style had always been divisive. Some – like Michael Gove and Boris Johnson – deferred to Cummings's planet-sized brain. Others, like David Cameron, considered him politically toxic.

Cummings says, 'Bernard suddenly blurted out in a meeting about various tensions in the operation, "You're in completely the wrong role. I don't think you should have a management role any more. Matthew is the great manager."'

'Bernard, you don't know anything about me,' said Cummings. 'The main thing I do is managing things. What do you think my job is?'

'Your job is being on the phone to journalists all day,' said Jenkin.

'That's less than 5 per cent of my time. Most of what I'm doing is building a team and managing a team. That's what I did at the Department of Education.'

'My proposal is that Dominic should be removed from any actual management position,' said Jenkin. John Mills, a Eurosceptic Labour donor and then deputy chairman of Vote Leave, and Matthew Elliott both looked startled.

Matthew told Jenkin, 'Bernard, that's mad.'

'Why?' asked Bernard.

'If Dominic left, almost everyone through that glass window would go.'

Cummings recalls thinking at the time: 'Elliott actually understands his position. That's good. That means he's much less likely to fuck up.'

As he now accepts, 'This suckered me into a false sense of confidence, as it turned out in January [when the second coup attempt took place].'

According to Cummings, Daniel Hannan, the Conservative MEP, also backed the coup. Cummings reports Hannan saying to him during the coup, 'It's your patriotic duty to resign and go over to the campaign, and tell them you're leaving because Mary's pregnant. And tell them it's their patriotic duty to stay and work with Matthew Elliott.'

'Dan Hannan said I was being unpatriotic,' confirms Victoria Woodcock. 'I said I was being patriotic. Because, without Dom, we couldn't win the referendum.'

'At that point, Matthew had given up on the coup,' says Dominic Cummings.

He said, 'Dan, forget it.'

Once the coup didn't happen, Dan was in a sticky position. He knew what he'd said to me, what he'd said to the others.

Still, he's sort of a hero. He was right about the referendum. He suffered a lot of mockery. Cameron told him he was on the wrong side of history. He's been vindicated.

Daniel Hannan, meanwhile, insists he didn't want to lose Cummings, but that he wanted to modify his role.

'Some people wanted to get rid of him,' says Hannan.

He was rubbing some MPs up the wrong way, and MPs can be a precious lot. But I was terrified that he might leave altogether.

He is brilliant at strategy. I wanted him to stay but subject to constraint. It made sense to ask him to stop tweeting. There was no point in him tweeting how clever his strategy was – it only put more information the other side's way.

As the coup ran out of steam, Chris Grayling was still sending text messages to Matthew Elliott.

'Matthew came over to me, showing me his text messages from Grayling,' says Cummings. 'The texts said, "I can't believe you've all bottled it. You must press on."

'Matthew was in such a state, he was showing me texts, saying, "How should I reply?"

'I was dictating Elliott's replies to Grayling, with Dan running around, trying to get the coup restarted.'

The rebellion quickly collapsed, like an ageing soufflé. At the next Vote Leave board meeting, it was confirmed that Cummings would run the campaign for the next five months, right up until referendum day.

CHAPTER 5

FARAGE ON THE CAMPAIGN TRAIL

The best referendum strategy for Farage was the simplest one – get him out on the streets, day after day.

'It involved an element of risk,' he says. 'When you meet real people, some of them call you a "see you next Tuesday". I couldn't care less. Everyone else is so risk averse, they won't do it.'

Farage advised Donald Trump to take a similar approach in the American elections, when he addressed a Trump rally in Mississippi in August 2016.

'I saw him with the activists – there was something of a feel that he was running his campaign like we do our stuff, mobilising the grassroots,' says Farage. 'I said, "Get your walking boots on."'

'I did a private event with him first, for fifty Mississippi donors – $50,000 donors type, not really big in American terms. I watched him interacting with them, lining up to do photographs. He was good with them.'

UKIP also depended on blitzing the local media, getting out and meeting people, activating people at rallies and mo- bilising a volunteer army, particularly in regional cities.

'The irony of Vote Leave is that, without UKIP, they wouldn't have had a campaign anyway – because on the ground it was all our people,' says Nigel Farage. 'Our people had different badges on – UKIP badges on, GO badges, Vote Leave badges on.'

This is a rare occasion that Daniel Hannan and Farage agreed with one another.

'The foot soldiers of the campaign from UKIP were models of disinterested patriotism,' says Hannan. 'No one could have worked harder than they did.'

Farage concentrated not only on the north, but also on specific regions in the north, to catch the regional news.

'The best days on the road, we were hitting the half past six regional news in two regions: the Midlands and the north,' he says.

There was a massive focus on local media – they were des- perate for something interesting. Whatever Remain were doing, with their stalls and leaflets and online, they weren't [reaching regional news].

When we were in Sheffield, it was as if we were the first people to turn up and do anything. Bolton was the same – it wasn't happening. We were making a story for them. The local media were going mad for it, the local independent radio stations, the local press. It's like there are two medias

– well, there are three [including social media] – that are desperate for real stuff.

'What was amazing in the referendum campaign was to see a national conversation going on around dull as ditchwater press conferences in Millbank Tower [just by Westminster, on the banks of the Thames],' continues Farage. 'It's of no interest to anybody.'

Individual Conservative MPs, such as Sir Bill Cash, also took to campaigning on their own.

'There was a concern among individual MPs about the Vote Leave campaign literature,' says Sir Bill. 'We had our own network. It was rather like a general election, with a mutual awareness of what was needed in the national interest.'

Remain, too, was extremely busy, campaigning on the streets.

'Believe you me, one of the great shocks to me was how active on the ground Remain were,' says Farage.

I hadn't read it. I hadn't seen it. They had the Liberal Democrats completely on board. And the Lib Dem activist base is still there. They may have lost their national appeal, but they still want to win councils.

They also had all the paid staff that worked for the Labour Party, that worked for the Conservative Party, some of the trade unionists. They were much more active on the ground in terms of leafleting than we were.

What Remain could not do was the rallies. They didn't

have the people who would get an audience. Lord Mandelson, with the greatest of respect, would not get a big crowd to turn out. They also were very big on social media. They segmented very cleverly. They'd go for football supporters. They fought a very sophisticated campaign.

Chris Bruni-Lowe, Nigel Farage and Arron Banks did everything they could to build up coverage to rival Vote Leave's.

'Arron Banks was slightly Trumpesque: shout, shout, shout, to get parity,' says Bruni-Lowe.

For three or four months, every time Vote Leave went on, Nigel went on. It was absolutely planned. We got Nigel to do weekly speeches in Westminster to explain how Leave can win: he talked about immigration, Turkey and the Australian points system. We knew it would cause Vote Leave palpitations. But we wanted to get them into gear, to promote the issues.

That's the big question of the Leave campaign. Did the mutual competition – and loathing – of the different Leave factions spur them on to greater success? Or might they have done even better if their principal figureheads hadn't been knocking seven bells out of each other?

'I don't think the Leave campaign was badly split – the competition was great,' says Bruni-Lowe.

Elliott is a very bad campaigner. He had no ground campaign;

he didn't do the streets, but UKIP does. If Arron Banks can do a serious street campaign, then Elliott, to win designation, would have to do the same thing. Yes, you're at loggerheads. But you've got two sets of campaigns spending shedloads of money in different parts of the country.

In this byzantine game of electoral chess, it seemed crazy at the time that the various Leave groups didn't coalesce; not least since Remain looked far more unified. I was told on several occasions that some members of Vote Leave were keen to unify, but not at the cost of Nigel Farage being the head of the coalition – which, some said, was his cast-iron condition. Farage denies this outright.

'The [Vote Leave] idea was to damage me as much as possible,' he says. 'The amount they invested in trying to damage me was unbelievable. I'm toxic… all that. These are really very unpleasant human beings.'

Farage was incensed, too, that immigration wasn't the number one issue for Vote Leave.

'What was just ridiculous was this Hannan/Carswell view that open-door immigration is great and that, actually, if we discuss the subject at all, we'd put off people,' says Farage. 'Well, we'd put off people at their Notting Hill dinner parties but it's just not the way politics is. It's very odd that they simply couldn't see that.'

And so, from January till May 2016, Nigel Farage continued to push on immigration while Vote Leave steered clear of it until the closing stages of the campaign.

'A lot of the effort was to force the immigration issue and talk about Turkey,' says Chris Bruni-Lowe.

> Vote Leave kept on saying it was toxic. Our view was that if we can use immigration to turn out the vote in Boston and Clacton, we'll win. Their view was that we must suppress the vote by talking about the NHS.
>
> Nigel said, 'If you are playing in your own half the whole time, you'll get beaten. You've got to play on the front foot.'
>
> If Nigel is on the *Andrew Marr Show* in the final week, talking about the economy, we're finished. You've got to talk about immigration, you've got to make it uncomfortable.

Farage's opponents at Vote Leave thought that, if Farage was on the *Marr Show* talking about anything at all, then they didn't stand a chance.

I put to Farage the Farage Paradox – the more popular he, UKIP and the anti-immigration message grew, the more he put off the middle ground, and the more he decreased the chances of Brexit.

'Bollocks, absolute cock,' says Farage. 'They weren't going to work with us. It was as simple as that. They were stuck in this mentality that the UKIP element would put people off. Well, it's cock.'

When Farage swears, which he does often, there is no malice, but the choice of swearwords is old-fashioned.

'All you get from those careerists is a bunch of lies,' he says. 'No one tried harder than me to form the big umbrella – which I thought was the right approach. And I tried.'

The loathing between UKIP and Vote Leave was mutual, and considerable. UKIP were convinced Vote Leave was a largely Conservative outfit.

'It was about Conservative succession, it was about who was in No. 10, who got the jobs after the referendum – even the Labour Party left them,' says Farage, referring to John Mills, the businessman who had been deputy chairman of Vote Leave but left the organisation on 28 April 2016.

The different strands of the Leave movement are difficult to follow, sometimes attracting each other, sometimes repelling each other with great force. The complication was intensified by the desire to set up lots of different splinter groups – a phenomenon nicknamed 'Skateboarders for Nazis', to mock the attempts to get unlikely groups to back Brexit.

'Elliott is obsessed with American campaigns – women for Obama, Hispanics for Obama, men for Obama,' says Chris Bruni-Lowe. 'He wanted bikers for Britain, farmers for Britain, business for Britain. His view was, if we do it like this, we don't have to get in the Eurosceptic, toxic groups.'

Both Cleo Watson and Elliott had worked in America at the time of Barack Obama's 2012 re-election. And the Obama scheme was indeed followed. When I interviewed Matthew Elliott in the old Vote Leave offices on the South Bank in September 2016, there were still posters around the office, reading, 'Women for Britain', 'Historians for Britain', 'Muslims for Britain' and 'Farmers for Britain'.

'Plus Vote Leave didn't understand what the issues were to win the referendum until quite late,' says Chris Bruni-Lowe.

> In the end, they understood it, they got it. Farage accepts that he is loathed by many voters – and realised there was no point in appealing to them.
>
> If you want to win everyone over, Nigel will never do that. If you want to motivate those who want to leave, and piss off Lib Dems and those that want to Remain, he'll do that.

Farage cheerfully accepts how much he is disliked by many people.

'The point is that, for those that were always going to vote Remain, the more they see of me, the less they like me. But that doesn't matter, does it?' he says. 'Rather like the Cameron strategy of being nice to the *Guardian* readers in 2005. Great. They're not going to vote for you anyway. What's the point? This is not a beauty contest. It's a hard-nosed game of getting numbers.'

Cameron would argue that it was the other way round. He knew he had the votes of Middle England in the bag; better to let them hold their noses and vote for him, while still appealing to the centre-left. It meant he was often hated by Tories. The vigour of the hatred was often surprising, usually from those of his own class and background, who saw him as a traitor; unlike moderate Tories, who tended to rather like him.

As the referendum campaign got going in early 2016, the mutual loathing between Farage and Vote Leave snowballed.

In a titanic game of handbags at five paces, both sides accused the other of wanting to lose, or preparing to lose.

'They thought we'd lose from the start,' says Farage about Vote Leave. 'They wanted a noble loss. The paranoid fear they had was me playing a big role in the referendum and 30 per cent of the Conservative Party being irreconcilable to a Cameron campaign that kept Britain in the European Union, and UKIP reaping a massive benefit, SNP-style.'

And so Farage ended up operating as a separate entity from Vote Leave, travelling all over the country.

'Our view was, now we've got to turn the vote out,' says Bruni-Lowe.

Ship Nigel up and down the country in every working-class town, where there was no Labour campaign. If you can motivate Out voters, you can win. That's why turnout was 76 per cent in Boston, 75 per cent in Essex. The Remain side weren't so enthusiastic. Their enthusiasm has come after the referendum.

Farage was happy to share a stage with any Eurosceptic, however unappetising their politics.

'At the event we did in Belfast, we had people on that platform that wanted to kill each other,' says Farage. 'We had Republicans, and we had some ultra-Unionists and they all sat on a stage together.'

Farage realised that, unlike in a first-past-the-post general election, every vote did count, whether it came from a naturally Europhile area or a staunch Eurosceptic one. Thus his decision to stand on a platform with George Galloway, who puts many voters off but appeals strongly to a small constituency.

'It was important to get George,' he says. 'I think he did twenty public meetings round the country. He did one in Walthamstow to 2,000 people – a big mosque.'

Farage also wanted to align with prominent Eurosceptics who were otherwise far removed from him politically. Before the 2014 death of Bob Crow, the hard-left general secretary of the RMT, Farage had planned a Eurosceptic tour with him.

'I already had a deal with Bob Crow, some years ago, that we would tour Britain, we would campaign round Britain, we would speak round Britain and we would drink round Britain,' says Farage. 'He, of all the trade union leaders of the last few years, ticks all the boxes of an old-style trade union leader. We would have done a double act round the country. I couldn't do that with George Galloway.'

Farage also mourns the loss of 'dear old Tony Benn', another far-left Eurosceptic, who also died in 2014.

One far-left Eurosceptic who would really have helped Farage's cause was Jeremy Corbyn, who has spent most of his life attacking Europe, before leadership of the Labour Party made him change his tune.

'I'm sure he did [vote for Brexit] – he was the great loss to our side,' says Farage. 'Had Corbyn backed our side of the campaign, we'd have won by a far bigger margin. He would have been very important. We knew that last June from our polling.'

All the same, Corbyn's apathetic approach to the EU did Leave a considerable favour.

'He's just a hypocrite,' says Farage. 'The irony is, the higher his profile was for Remain, the more the entire Establishment laughed their socks off, at a man who'd been against it for thirty years. Isn't it funny? He gets condemned for being low profile. Theresa May gets lauded. Work that out.'

'Corbyn being lukewarm was very useful,' says Douglas Carswell.

It confirmed what a lot of people suspected – there's a very powerful left-wing argument against the EU. It made people realise you don't have to be a Tory, let alone UKIP, to want democracy.

Gisela Stuart was probably the single most important asset. The fact that she's a first-generation Briton from Germany – so reasonable and not what Eurosceptics are supposed to be – is a magnificent antidote. She's wonderful.

Corbyn's half-hearted approach to Remain also annoyed David Cameron and George Osborne.

'He was positively distracting,' says one of Osborne's senior advisers. 'He calculated that it was in his interest not to be too Europhile. A lot of the key voters in the end were Labour voters, while a lot of Tory constituencies voted in.'

Labour consistently misjudged the taste for Brexit among

a big proportion of their voters – a taste that led voters not only to vote Leave in the referendum, but also to vote UKIP in the 2015 general election.

'We always assumed that Ed Miliband would concede a referendum, with support [for a referendum] sky high in the seats he needs to win,' says Douglas Carswell.

> He doesn't, and look at the result. This has been skated over. People assume that Miliband lost because he couldn't eat a bacon sandwich gracefully, or some such nonsense. We've seriously neglected the extent to which the Labour Party lost the general election and lost it badly because they refused to concede a referendum.

It wasn't just the Labour Party that was riven with division. So was UKIP – and it has remained deeply split since the referendum, as its MEPs get into fist fights and its leaders come and go at alarming speed. As the referendum loomed closer into view, Douglas Carswell noticed some UKIP MEPs were indifferent about whether they actually won the referendum.

'I was having a lot of conversations with a lot of MEPs in UKIP, in the run-up to designation, where they'd admit to me that, if the wrong people were put in charge of the referendum campaign, it would make leaving the EU less likely,' Carswell says.

> But they were quite cheerful about this because they thought, in the best-case scenario – senior UKIP figures would say to

my face – 'If we narrowly lose the referendum, it would allow us to do in England what the SNP did in Scotland. People would feel aggrieved and would push all those Leave voters to UKIP.'

In other words, according to Carswell, UKIP were trying to emulate the SNP and maintain a public profile, without achieving its central objective – while Vote Leave were intent on winning the actual thing.

'Only one UKIP MEP endorsed Vote Leave,' says Carswell.

Do you support a vehicle you can control that won't do the job or a vehicle that you can't control, that you'll be part of, that will get you the result you want? The overwhelming majority of UKIP MEPs, who've repeatedly stood for election, promising to get us out of Europe, chose the option that was less likely to get us out of Europe, and some said it would be a good thing.

So, in early 2016, the various Leave operations still looked like a bunch of mutually loathing ferrets.

February 2016 was the turning point. That was the month, Vote Leave insiders say, when everything changed. David Cameron came back from Brussels with a hollow deal – and Michael Gove and Boris Johnson entered the fray.

CHAPTER 6

BORIS IRONS THE KNICKERS WHILE GOVE MAKES THE SPEECHES

In his unpublished *Telegraph* article – written on 19 February but not leaked until 16 October – Boris Johnson argued that Britain should stay in Europe. He also made a rare classical mistake.

Boris wrote, 'Cameron was going to probe the belly of the beast and bring back British sovereignty, like Hercules bringing Eurydice back from the underworld.'

Boris was mixing up his myths. It was Orpheus who tried – and failed – to bring Eurydice back from the underworld. Hercules did go down to the underworld – to retrieve, successfully, the horrible, three-headed Cerberus.

It's very unlike Boris to get his classical myths muddled up – for all his carefully contrived bumbling, the classics is something he normally never gets wrong. It just goes to show what a panic he was in over the Europe question.

In fact, there was some serendipitous wisdom in his mistake; *se non è vero, è ben trovato.*

It would have taken the might of a Hercules to get the perfect deal out of Brussels. And, if Cameron had pulled off the perfect deal, it wouldn't have been a Cerberus – the monstrous Hound of Hades – he retrieved, but a beautiful, miraculous thing, just like Eurydice, the lovely oak nymph, a daughter of Apollo.

Actually, David Cameron came back with something that was more Cerberus than Eurydice. On 19 February 2016, he announced the limited concessions he'd squeezed out of the twenty-seven other EU leaders – on migration, benefits, euro safeguards, the working time directive, budgets, EU waste, child benefit, sham marriages, a red card for national parliaments, ever-closer union, security and a multi-currency union.

The reform was never going to be enough for Nigel Farage. Not that Farage was on the edge of his seat, waiting for David Cameron to come back with any reform of the EU – ever.

'There are no reforms possible,' Farage said. 'I'm one of the few people who would say that. There's been this fundamental misunderstanding of Europe post-Maastricht of where it was going.'

'We needed to say these reforms are rubbish,' says Chris Bruni-Lowe.

From May 2015 till December, we asked who was the most trusted leader, and it was always David Cameron.

After about Christmas, it bombed off a cliff because of the failed renegotiation. The public thought this was a put-up job. He went from one of the most popular to one of the most unpopular. That's why we were happy with Nigel going against Cameron. They [Remain] saw Cameron as a star figure. Actually, we viewed it completely opposite. You saw the audiences on telly, and they started bringing in other gripes – grammar schools, the NHS, education.

The feeling that Cameron had come back with nothing was universal among Eurosceptics.

'I don't think they even asked for the things Eurosceptics want,' says Douglas Carswell. 'They never made the effort to understand what Eurosceptics want. They always thought they were going to win.

'Cameron could have got associate membership. When the new team starts asking for these things, I suspect the officials will say, "Why didn't you ask for these things?"'

Dominic Cummings continued to run his focus groups. Cameron's failure to secure a deal had a huge effect on them.

One question asked whether people thought, A – the EU is a very good thing and I'll vote Remain; B – the EU is rubbish and I'll vote Leave; C – I don't like the EU but I'm worried about leaving.

Before Cameron came back with his deal, the figures were around a third, a third and a fifth for A, B and C respectively, with another 10–15 per cent not interested. Those figures had stayed roughly consistent for months, until Cameron came back with his deal, when the figure for Leave soared to 40 per cent.

'The deal was one of Cameron's biggest fuck-ups,' says Dominic Cummings.

> The single biggest issue was immigration, and the deal didn't touch it.
>
> He was persuaded by Ed Llewellyn [Cameron's chief of staff] about what was possible. Lots of people – including friends of Cameron – said, 'This deal is pretty threadbare, mate.' Very quickly, the word came down from Cameron himself, 'This is a bloody great deal. No one goes into meetings and says this is a bad deal.'
>
> When Michael [Gove] had his big conversation with him – 'I've got some serious problems with it' – he wouldn't hear it. He launched into, 'This is why the deal is brilliant, wankers in the media are wrong.'
>
> Michael thinks he persuaded himself that he had got some major concessions. A lot of people think Cameron must be a lying twat. I think Michael's more accurate – Cameron genuinely thought it was a good deal. But he only got a few tiny concessions.

Cameron's failure to bring back any significant reforms from Europe wasn't the only boost for the Brexit camp.

'At those Tate meetings, we realised we needed two things: one was for a major party leader to come over to our side; the other was for Cameron to come back from his negotiations with nothing,' says Hannan. 'Effectively, we ended up with both.'

Jeremy Corbyn was undeniably lacklustre during the Remain campaign. He did officially back Remain but was never very convincing – giving the EU only seven, or seven and a half, out of ten.

'You only have to look at his face as he comes out of the polling booth to realise that he voted Leave,' says Hannan.

February was a crucial month for Leave, then – with Cameron's failure to secure major concessions, which led to two big scalps for Vote Leave.

On 20 February 2016, Michael Gove came out for Leave. He had told David Cameron at Christmas that he would be voting Leave, but that he wouldn't become a senior campaigner. When he decided to campaign for Brexit hell-for-leather, it caused a split between the Goves and the Camerons that persists today.

'Michael was genuinely torn between friendship and belief,' says one of George Osborne's senior advisers. 'But, once you're in a campaign, you want to win.'

A day later, on 21 February, Boris Johnson followed suit and came out for Brexit. The announcements had been a long time coming.

'The core messages had been set by early 2016,' says Dominic Cummings.

The main issue was, 'Will Michael and Boris come to our side or not?'

I was very confident Michael would come over. One of the problems in the coup is I couldn't tell people that. I had a trump card to play but I couldn't play it. I couldn't overtly say, 'No one knows this, apart from me and Michael's wife.'

I could hint and say, which I did, 'We have to think there are a bunch of people, the two most important of which are Boris and Michael. Do you think that Michael Gove is more likely to join the campaign with Dominic Cummings as campaign director, or with Arron Banks and Andy Wigmore running the show? Forget whether you like me or not. What is more likely?'

If Banks and Wigmore are running it, Boris and Michael are much more likely to say, 'No way.'

Boris was never such a definite Leaver – as he showed in those two opposed columns for the *Telegraph*. That is typical Boris – typical of one who actually said, in that unpublished Remain column, 'Shouldn't our policy be like our policy on cake – pro having it and pro eating it? Pro Europe and pro the rest of the world?'

In this case, he really had to choose between having and eating.

Was Boris's heart ever deeply set on Brexit – or was his defection to the Out cause pure careerism, aimed at securing the leadership votes of Conservative members, who are three quarters Eurosceptic?

Douglas Carswell, the lone UKIP MP, spotted early signs

Boris was moving over to the Eurosceptic side for principled reasons. Just after Carswell won the Clacton by-election on 9 October 2014, he was on the *Andrew Marr Show* with Johnson – and the rock star Bryan Adams. At one point in the green room, Carswell took a selfie with Adams, much to the consternation of Adams's PR.

'His PR was saying, "Are you sure? This guy's UKIP,"' says Carswell, 'And Bryan said, "Yeah, whatever."'

Carswell then started chatting with Boris.

'I realised we thought much the same,' says Carswell.

> We talked about immigration and I said, 'Free movement of people and labour mobility are going to become more important, and not to be feared.'
>
> He said, 'Oh, so you're not anti-immigrants at all. You're anti-uncontrolled immigration.' I remember thinking he's not that far away from me either. He didn't come out for Vote Leave for personal gain.

In his heart, Boris is a Europhile. As he himself has written, 'Look, I'm rather pro-European, actually. I certainly want a European community where one can go off and scoff croissants, drink delicious coffee, learn foreign languages and generally make love to foreign women.'

This push-me-pull-you approach to the EU was played out during the campaign. Even on the eve of coming out for the Leave side, he was dithering. Moments before making his first Leave speech, he texted David Cameron, saying Brexit would be 'crushed like the toad beneath the harrow' – a line from the Rudyard Kipling poem 'Pagett, MP':

> The toad beneath the harrow knows
> Exactly where each tooth-point goes.

Senior Europhile Tories remain convinced that Boris never was a Eurosceptic.

'He joined Vote Leave entirely for leadership reasons,' says one of George Osborne's senior advisers.

> He didn't want to leave the EU; he told George that. He was flirting with the idea of a second referendum. By definition, that means he didn't want to leave. He didn't think Leave would win. It was a bet to nothing. He wouldn't disappoint his Eurosceptic supporters and Britain would stay in the EU.

Boris may be at heart an internationalist and a Europhile. But his spell reporting for the *Telegraph* in Brussels meant he saw the shortcomings of the EU up close. His head swayed his heart – and it helped, of course, that declaring himself a Leaver increased his chances of becoming Prime Minister.

He is also a gambler and a rebel by nature.

Boris's sister, Rachel Johnson, told me, 'Brexit attracts rebels with the light of distant horizons in their eyes who hate being told what to do, who probably had dominant fathers or bullying headmasters. Bremainers are risk-averse, keep-a-hold-of-nurse prefects.'

In this respect, Boris's character could hardly be more different from David Cameron's. And it is through the prism of their different characters that you can see why these two Conservatives – who share so many political views – were divided by Europe. And you can see why, in the end, the gambling outsider beat the patrician safe pair of hands.

Boris is certainly an unbiddable rebel, his eyes illuminated by the not-so-distant horizon of Downing Street.

Throw in the divorce of Boris's parents when he was a teenager and you build a fuller picture of his character: independent, tough, driven, risk-taking.

These things explain why Boris – for all the hyper-English, Wodehousian quotes and the Churchill and Shakespeare biographies, for all the Eton and Oxford education – is something of an outsider; and why he bet it all on the gamble of Brexit.

Meanwhile, Cameron's childhood was rooted in the happy marriage of his parents and a never-changing home – his mother and older brother, Alexander Cameron QC, still live in Peasemore, Berkshire, where the Camerons grew up.

Cameron is by no means a wallflower – his confidence is considerable. But that safe-as-houses background and his extremely strong marriage have forged his steady-as-she-goes, pragmatic, undogmatic, dutiful politics.

They served him well, making him the greatest Tory election winner since Margaret Thatcher was turfed out of office twenty-six years ago. But they also meant he was inclined to cleave to Europe rather than take the gamble on Brexit. The division on Brexit was as much about character as politics.

Not everyone was so enamoured with Boris's attachment to Vote Leave.

Dominic Cummings recalls, 'Bernard Jenkin said to me, "I don't think Michael will come over. But, if he does come over, Boris will come over and that will be a disaster."'

'Why is it a disaster for the most popular politician in Britain to be on our side?' asked Cummings.

'He's dishonest, a philanderer.'

In fact, Boris turned out to be a boost to the Vote Leave campaign, a fact Nigel Farage acknowledges. Of all his fellow Brexiteers, Farage speaks most generously of Johnson and Kate Hoey.

'There was also a chronic misunderstanding, from a Leave perspective, of how few people could reach the electorate,' says Farage.

> The political figures that could reach a significant number of people were four or five. Me, Boris, Gove scraping it, Kate Hoey, who is far bigger than Gisela Stuart.
>
> Gisela was unknown. You can't just become known. Kate Hoey's been around for thirty years. She's been sports minister. Getting well known in politics is about drip on the stone. One day, ten years ago, people knew who I was. They hadn't the day before. It takes time.

The arrival of Gove and Johnson energised the Vote Leave campaign – particularly in the case of Boris, the only politician who doubles as a full-blown celeb. Douglas Carswell tells a self-deprecating story about getting out of a battle bus at a town meeting where they were expecting Boris. He could feel a palpable collapse of excitement as it became clear no blond superstar was jumping off the bus behind him.

'The arrival of Boris and Gove was amazing,' says Carswell.

I knew they were going to come out but there were delays. It was like the cavalry arriving. I knew people would be coming – I had an inkling who they might be. Michael I was always pretty sure of.

My job was to manage the UKIP flank. When the cavalry arrived, everyone focused on the cavalry. It was Dan [Hannan], Dom [Cummings] and Matt [Elliott] who made sure there were masses of infantry ready. They used the internet to create a pop-up party. It shifted vast amounts of literature. It created a presence in the nooks and crannies of Britain and, like many pop-up parties, it went when it had done its job.

Given what was to transpire between them, Gove and Johnson hit it off surprisingly well on the campaign trail.

'Gove and Boris worked very well together,' says Douglas Carswell.

Everyone put aside all sorts of differences at every level. Dan and Dominic and Matt set the example from the top. There was this culture in Vote Leave that we were all embarking on this endeavour.

Dan, Dom, Michael Gove, Boris, Gisela were making the key decisions. It's the only campaign I've ever fought where I stuck to the line I was told to take – often by guys who had been out to get me during the general election.

I'd be asked to do an interview. If they say, 'Don't do it', I didn't do it, talk about something else. They might say, 'We'll get Andrea Leadsom on instead of you.' I was happy. I wasn't going to shift opinion the way others do.

Vote Leave got another boost on 13 April 2016, when it won official designation from the Electoral Commission as the principal leave campaign. This allowed them to spend up to £7 million on the campaign, as well as send out free mailshots and get guaranteed TV election broadcasts. This led to more bad blood between the Leave groups, with Leave.EU backer Arron Banks threatening a court case to review the designation decision.

'The thing that swung designation was the Cabinet ministers [backing Vote Leave],' says Chris Bruni-Lowe. 'The Electoral Commission couldn't turn against the Establishment. In some ways, Vote Leave was better. They had more staff. Arron Banks didn't have enough staff.'

In the end, Banks accepted the decision without an appeal, Vote Leave retained designation and the different groups mounted their own separate campaigns, overlapping on the occasions when the principal combatants didn't happen to loathe each other.

At this stage, Gove and Boris were working happily under the direction of Dominic Cummings.

'Michael's approach all the way through was, "I want to help you guys win, and I'll do what you tell me to do,"' says Dominic Cummings.

> Boris was also very good: 'I'm here to help you. You guys are in charge. You tell me what to do.'
>
> During the campaign, we'd developed this structure round Boris and Michael. Boris was very good. Only once did we have hard words in four months – over the ITV thing.

On 11 May, ITV announced that Nigel Farage would be appearing in the same programme as David Cameron, if not actually debating against him.

Dominic Cummings – horrified that the potentially toxic Farage would dominate proceedings – sent this email to journalists:

> The establishment has tried everything from spending taxpayers' money on pro-EU propaganda to funding the In campaign via Goldman Sachs. The polls have stayed fifty-fifty. They're now fixing the debates to shut out the official campaign.
>
> ITV is led by people like Robert Peston who campaigned for Britain to join the euro. ITV has lied to us in private while secretly stitching up a deal with Cameron to stop Boris Johnson or Michael Gove debating the issues properly.
>
> ITV has effectively joined the official In campaign and there will be consequences for its future – the people in No. 10 won't be there for long.

Commentators have suggested this was a sign of Cummings planning a job with Gove in Downing Street. He denies this; in fact, it was Cummings's shot across the BBC's bows – to stop them doing a similar deal in their debates.

'Some people said Dom had blown it with his reaction to ITV colluding with Downing Street to decide who the Leave spokesman was,' says Douglas Carswell.

> I was absolutely livid. We had to go overboard – to make it clear to the people at the BBC that there would be consequences.
>
> Dominic was right to escalate it to a major confrontational issue. If the BBC had caved in, if Nigel had been the spokesman in every debate, we'd have lost.
>
> If Vote Leave had been allowed to run the campaign, without Downing Street and ITV [colluding], if one or two senior UKIP figures hadn't spent months trying to undermine Dominic and Matt, we'd have won 60–40.

When Boris Johnson heard about the Vote Leave statement on the ITV decision about Farage, he was alarmed.

Dominic Cummings recalls, 'He said, "What the fuck are you doing, threatening to take out Peston? Jesus Christ, Dominic!"

'I said, "I should have called you." He was cross. At the end of it, he was fine.'

As the campaign progressed, relations between Cummings and Boris improved drastically. And Gove and Boris got on increasingly well, too, not least because they were different from the other MPs working for the Leave vote.

'At the campaign committee meetings, lots of the MPs, apart from Gove and Boris, would say, "You fucked this up! Why am I not on TV?"' says Dominic Cummings. 'These situations are so strange and the people are so dreadful – the ridiculous narcissism. Both Boris and Michael realise the absurdity of the whole thing, which very few people do. They can both sit back and laugh at things, and laugh with each other.'

Still, it was only in mid-May that the public really began to be galvanised by the referendum.

'Most people aren't paying any attention to anything until the last minute,' says Dominic Cummings. 'A week before Cameron came back with the deal in February, people weren't zoned into it at all. In the vast majority of the period from May 2015, there is no attention. Then there's a massive focus in the last six weeks.'

Gove and Johnson grew even closer on 17 May, when a story was leaked to *The Sun*, wrongly suggesting that Boris's wife, Marina Wheeler, was the mystery QC caught having sex with another lawyer outside Waterloo Station, in an incident which had been reported to the police by passers-by. The rumour is that the leak came from government, and more specifically the office of George Osborne. Osborne's allies strongly deny this.

'It's certainly not true,' says one of Osborne's senior advisers. 'George gets accused of all sorts of things that aren't true.

As a Machiavelli, you get attributed with powers and skills you don't have.'

Whoever was responsible for the story, it had a galvanising effect on Boris.

'Boris and Michael definitely became much closer friends during the campaign, particularly when the government launched those attacks,' says Dominic Cummings. 'Michael, who'd said I'd been too tough on them, said, "They've behaved disgracefully. I've got to support Boris."'

Boris was infuriated by the lie about his wife.

'That was a massive fuck-up by the government; it massively played into my hands,' says Dominic Cummings. 'There were a whole bunch of stories against Boris that week. *The Sun* splashed on it. Boris came into my office and said, "I thought these were my friends. They are out to kill me. We've got to win."'

Boris is certainly no innocent – but he is free from malice. He likes to think the best of people, and he wouldn't have wanted to believe that Cameron and Osborne were out to destroy him. That's not how he sees the world.

'As the campaign started, lots of people told Boris, "Osborne's out to destroy you,"' says Cummings. 'He said, "Nooo, it's all media nonsense."'

'Boris certainly thought the story came from Osborne. It turned out to be enormously self-destructive for them. His immediate reaction was, "We've got to fucking win."'

Michael Gove, too, jumped to Boris's defence.

Dominic Cummings remembers:

I said to Michael, 'They're going for Boris. They're going to come for you and say, "Stay out of it." You've got to publicly defend him and privately support him.'

Michael said, 'Absolutely. This is terrible behaviour from them. And I am going to support Boris.' And he did. Privately, he said, 'What No. 10 has done is deplorable. I assume David and George don't know about this. But this must be stopped and this is why we must win.'

They both got closer all the way through to the day.

The government had met its Waterloo. For the first six weeks of the campaign, Johnson and Gove had pulled their punches. After the leaked story, they were up for the battle.

Cummings told Johnson:

> Boris, I've been telling you and Michael that, if you want to win, you have to pick up a baseball bat and smash David Cameron and George Osborne over the head on the subject of money, the NHS and immigration. It's very simple. If you do that, you will win. If you don't, you might lose, you will probably lose.

With the money that was enabled by designation, Vote Leave could use other outlets, too. They delivered 15 million leaflets through their activists, and another 40 million through the postal service. Meanwhile, in April 2016, the government sent out Remain leaflets to 27 million homes. As a stunt, Chris Bruni-Lowe got Farage to post his own government Remain leaflet back through the door of No. 10.

Alongside Vote Leave's leafleting and online electioneering, Boris became their chief public face.

Dominic Cummings says, 'The terrible mistake that Downing Street made of going after Boris personally was Boris then said, "What have we got to do to win?"'

Cummings told him he should front the news on immigration statistics. Boris proceeded to do exactly that.

'Boris then says, "I want to write a letter to the Prime Minister and Osborne, signed by me, Michael and Gisela – a good way to keep the story going to the Sundays,"' says Cummings.

This letter, published in the *Sunday Times* on 29 May 2016, called on Cameron to end his pledge to limit net migration to tens of thousands a year because it was impossible to achieve while within the EU.

Cummings drafted the letter.

'Boris comes back, says, "Excellent, excellent,"' recalls Cummings. 'He then said, "I think there should be a line there that says it's corrosive and undermines public trust."'

The line that did eventually appear in the letter reads: 'This promise is plainly not achievable as long as the UK is a member of the EU and the failure to keep it is corrosive of public trust in politics.'

'Michael said, "I'm not sure." Boris says, "It's true. This bullshit promise of 100,000 [net immigrants to Britain a year] has been corrosive. We've got to tell the truth."

'Michael buckles down. Gisela says, "I completely agree." It's the splash in the *Sunday Times*. All hell breaks loose.'

From then on, Johnson and Gove were fully with the programme, agreeing to everything Vote Leave lined up for them each day.

'That week happens and all the polls start shifting,' says Cummings. 'It's a combination of immigration, money, NHS and fuel bills. By the next weekend, the polls start moving. Through the next week, they keep moving.'

So Johnson and Gove were getting on like a house on fire. Who'd have thought that, barely a month later, the Chuckle Brothers of Vote Leave would be torn asunder?

Well, Nigel Farage, for one. He says he spotted Gove on manoeuvres a month before the vote.

'About five weeks before the referendum, we all said to each other here, "No, no. This isn't about Boris any more,"' says Farage. 'The only person who didn't see it was Boris. Basically, they sent Boris off on a bus to go and iron knickers in factories and they left Michael to do all the press stuff. It was so obvious. And who was running the campaign? Cummings.'

Farage is referring to the visit Boris made on 16 May 2016, to the David Nieper womenswear factory in Alfreton, Derbyshire. At one moment, he started ironing a Vote Leave banner, if not an actual pair of knickers.

In his speech, Johnson said to the workers:

When you look at the EU now, it makes me think of some badly designed undergarment which has now become too tight in some places – far too tight, far too constrictive – and dangerously loose in other places. Is that the kind of undergarment we make here at David Nieper? Absolutely not, absolutely not.

I just say to all those who prophesy gloom and doom for British business, I say their pants are on fire. If they want a new pair this is the place to come. Knickers to the pessimists!

Farage thinks the knickers factory visit was part of a concerted Gove campaign to relegate Boris to the second division.

'I noticed Gove was doing the more serious stuff while Boris was kept on the bus,' says Farage.

I could see the pattern and there was plenty of buzz about it from the Vote Leave campaign. There were games within a game. I wasn't a bit surprised when Gove decided to run. I actively thought he would. The extraordinary thing is that Boris didn't know or suspect a thing.

At one point, Farage even advised Gove to go for the leadership.

'He said, "I'll have to consult,"' says Farage. 'He meant with evil Cummings. "You don't have to consult," I said. "You could be the fucking PM."'

That said, Farage thought Boris was a boost to the campaign even while ironing knickers, or Vote Leave banners.

'I still think Boris was really important in the campaign – he reaches out,' says Farage.

They could have got him doing more exciting stuff.

The people who were very good were David Davis and Liam Fox. I shared platforms with them from Scotland to the West Country. Chris Grayling was great. I spoke to him a lot on the phone. It was the only time Grayling will ever get cheered in Stoke! Davis was happy to do anything. I spoke in Fox's constituency.

The UKIP team were mystified that Gove was used so prominently by Vote Leave. In September 2016, Chris Bruni-Lowe, Nigel Farage's chief pollster, did some polling for Survation, a market research agency. The poll asked, 'Who was the one figure in the campaign who made you most want to leave?' Gove was on 3 per cent, Farage on 29 per cent and Boris on 27 per cent.

'Why would Vote Leave use the most unpopular politician in Britain – Michael Gove – particularly unpopular among Labour voters, teachers, the left?' says Bruni-Lowe. 'I remember saying to Nigel on the phone, "There's something amiss here. Why are they making Boris iron knickers in factories? He should be doing the razzmatazz."'

Bruni-Lowe suggested a combined tour with Nigel Farage, Boris Johnson and Kate Hoey, taking in five cities in five days.

'It would have done it,' says Bruni-Lowe,

but Gove wanted to do it instead of Boris, I'm told. Every time we talked to Boris, he said, 'I want to do it but I'm being told it will damage my leadership chances.'

Nigel went to see Gove, and he was perfectly happy to do

it. What we now know, talking to lots of people, was that it was all about getting Gove in a position to run, from months out.

Snappers were saying to me, 'Get Farage and Boris together – it would be on the cover of every national newspaper.' They get on personally. But Vote Leave wouldn't allow it.

Not everyone agrees with the idea that Gove was on manoeuvres. Vote Leave insiders say Gove and Johnson did the speeches they felt they were best suited to deliver. That meant Gove, as Lord Chancellor, dealing with some of the more technical legal issues, and Boris plumping for lighter fare.

Both Johnson and Gove were happy to be briefed by Vote Leave analysts before television appearances – but Gove was particularly good at deferring to the analysts, carefully listening to them and absorbing large quantities of information.

'I know Michael – and I do not believe he was positioning himself [for leadership],' says Victoria Woodcock, who was a Gove adviser when he was Chief Whip and later joined his leadership campaign. 'He's not like that. He did believe that Cameron should stay afterwards.'

Once Gove knifed Johnson, after the referendum, Boris loyalists were also convinced Gove had been orchestrating a coup for a long time. And that meant a vicious, no-holds-barred, Mafioso hit on the blond – or the greased albino piglet, as his *Telegraph* colleagues nicknamed Boris, for his customary ability to shimmy away from blunders that would sink any other politician.

'George Osborne was part of the Gove plan – Gove spent the weekend at Dorneywood with Osborne a fortnight before he knifed [Johnson],' an old schoolfriend of Boris's says. 'They knew Boris would stand, and both Cameron and Osborne didn't want him to win.'

Dominic Cummings disagrees with this interpretation. Whatever the truth of Gove, Boris and the knickers factory, on 27 May, the government went into purdah – that is, the four-week period before referendum day when the government was banned from using the government machine to make the case for Remain.

Purdah didn't stop those last four weeks being the most tense, vicious and violent of the whole campaign.

CHAPTER 7

PROJECT FEAR: THE DOG THAT BARKED BUT DIDN'T BITE

When it became clear that David Cameron's Brussels deal wasn't going down well with the British public, Remain had to double down – and intensify their number one strategy: Project Fear.

On the Remain side, the tactics were dictated by David Cameron and George Osborne, even if they were nominally part of a larger Remain coalition. And those tactics largely consisted of keeping hold of nurse for fear of finding something worse.

That was not how it was planned initially by Britain Stronger in Europe – which was declared the official Remain campaign by the electoral commission on 13 April 2016.

'George Osborne did plan to promote positive aspects of the EU,' says one of Osborne's senior advisers.

There was a bigger argument about the security of Europe; that one of the positive advantages of Europe is that it locks people into peaceful union with each other. But the Brexit press parodied it as 'The EU stops World War Three'. In fact, that was the original purpose of the EU, despite the parody.

There were other positive messages, like the lower mobile phone charges introduced by the EU. But all that didn't have much traction with the public.

So the Remain campaign ended up being largely negative, built on the fear of the economic risks of leaving.

'In a campaign, you're not trying to persuade all the people,' says Osborne's adviser:

> 30 or 40 per cent are already on your side. You're only fo-cusing on the swing voter, who isn't convinced of the broad benefits of the EU. You'll find it hard to convince them with positive arguments. Leave used negative arguments as well – the dangers of millions of Turks coming here, of bankrupting the NHS. Their positive arguments were buried, too.

But negative arguments were more popularly associated with the Remain camp – thus the nickname, 'Project Fear', which was only used of Remain, however negative the Leave case may have been. Still, today, the Remain camp aren't entirely convinced Project Fear was such a bad idea.

'Of course there would be fiscal consequences of Brexit,' says Osborne's adviser.

You had to talk about the economic risks of leaving. Project

Fear didn't put voters off – focus groups and polling showed it had a good effect. It reminded people of the effects of leaving. Some people say, 'It was Project Fear wot won it.' That's crap. The arguments about economic risks kept Remain in it.

Unsurprisingly, that's not how the Brexiteers view Project Fear.

'Project Fear created such a sense of cynicism – it was almost childlike in its creation of ghosts,' says Sir Bill Cash, the Eurosceptic MP.

It became a joke. It was as if some manic Frankenstein had got some control of the bureaucracy. It was clearly coming from the government. How else did they get hold of figures like Christine Lagarde [managing director of the International Monetary Fund]? It was one form of unmitigated horror story after another. I can't believe anyone could believe it.

I had had a specific assurance from the Minister for Europe on the floor of the House that the information the government would supply under the Referendum Act would be accurate and impartial. The information was emphatically neither accurate nor impartial.

Dominic Cummings, who is never shy of criticising, is not entirely disparaging about the Remain campaign, or about Will Straw, Jack Straw's son, who ran the Britain Stronger in Europe group.

'Peter Mandelson and Amber Rudd were just getting on with their thing – it wasn't terribly run,' he says.

It's unfair to blame Will Straw; it's not his fault. The big decisions were taken by Cameron and Osborne.

The big mistakes were made by them. It's partly the extreme
negativity. Project Fear was right in principle but their tone
was so over the top, it backfired and undermined their own
credibility. My definite impression from market research was
that a gentle focus would have been more effective.

Cummings was confident, too, that few of the authority figures drafted in by Remain to attack Brexit would have an
effect on the poll.

'That's where Dominic [Cummings] was way ahead of
anyone else,' says Douglas Carswell.

I remember him saying, 'The IMF and these grandees can
pump out as many reports as they like. The only people who
can really harm us are Mark Carney [the Governor of the
Bank of England] – he's rated – and a couple of others.'

Carney was trusted. All the rest of them – the people
thought, 'They would say that, wouldn't they?'

This was what lay behind Michael Gove, in a Sky TV programme on 3 June, saying, 'People in this country have had
enough of experts.'

'Gove's point on experts was Cummings through and
through,' says Douglas Carswell.

Cummings, for his part, says, 'I didn't suggest to Michael
the experts line.'

He does acknowledge that Mark Carney was trusted. On 8 March, Carney warned of 'potential reduction in financial stability' as a result of a Brexit vote.

'Carney was bad for us, and good for them,' says Cummings. 'But they never hammered it home – some people had a vague idea. Of all the people they could have deployed, he was the most dangerous because of the brand – independent, Bank of England, [people think,] "They care about us."'

Remain leaders say it was inevitable that experts would come forward with their opinions.

'The Remain leaders didn't pick them,' says one of George Osborne's senior advisers.

Of course, the experts talked. It was the biggest economic issue at the time, and it still is. Of course, the OECD, the IMF and the rest of them are going to talk about it. Everyone said it was outrageous – but they have to talk about the elephant in the room.

We couldn't predict the effect of experts. There's randomness in the effect. Some expert might come out – and then Boris drops his ice cream and that becomes the story.

King of the doom-mongers was George Osborne, who said on 18 April that every family in Britain would be £4,300 worse off after a Brexit vote. On 14 June, he said there would have to be an 'Emergency Budget', nicknamed the Punishment Budget, with income tax going up by 2p.

'The one that I laughed my socks off [over] was to wake

up and be told that each family would be £4,300 worse off a year,' says Nigel Farage. 'I was in Bolton that day and they were saying, "I'm only earning twelve grand a year." That's why I said, just put a nought on the end. It was so ludicrous. There was quite a big Tory rebellion over the punishment budget.'

Farage is convinced Leave benefited from the Remain fear-mongering about the consequences of Brexit.

'They over-egged the pudding,' says Farage. 'The crucial moment was Obama.'

In a Foreign Office press conference with David Cameron on 22 April 2016, President Obama said Brexit Britain would be at the 'back of the queue' in any trade deal.

'You could see it in the polls very, very quickly – a 3 per cent swing in the undecided [towards Leave],' says Farage. 'There was a moment in that interview when just the look on Obama's face, when he talked about this country, [signalled,] "We're going to throw you off a cliff."'

The Vote Leave camp, too, were buoyed by the polls after Barack Obama's visit.

'I thought it would be bad,' says Douglas Carswell. 'I thought most people thought like I did – decent guy, friend of the country. Then you had a negative shift.'

Dominic Cummings had been tracking the Obama effect on the polls.

'Obama's intervention could have been harmful for us but they ended up overcooking it and it rebounded on them,' he says.

If you look at the average of the polls, it blips up the week before Obama, with 25 million households getting the document with the £4,300 figure [suggesting that's how much worse off Brexit would make them]. As soon as Obama happens, they go back to 50–50. The average of polls shows a fall. In focus groups, people react badly to Obama.

Scaremongering had been effective in both the 2014 Scottish referendum and the general election of 2015.

'There were parallels with the Scottish referendum,' says one of George Osborne's senior advisers. 'We were arguing for the status quo, which usually has its own attractions.'

Still, Remain had got into a negative habit – which didn't get traction when they were unable to sell the benefits of the EU.

'They got caught inside an electoral machine,' says Farage.

They had been wholly negative in Scotland and it probably had worked. The over-reliance on oil, the impossibility of asking the question of sterling versus the euro… I think in the end that cooked Salmond's goose.

In the general election, it probably worked. Crosby was utterly ruthless. They went down the same track. If it's worked twice, it's going to work again.

Sir Lynton Crosby, the Wizard of Oz, helped to win the 2015 election for the Tories. He had also been behind John Howard's four election wins in Australia between 1996 and 2004, as well as advising Boris Johnson on his two mayoral victories in 2008 and 2012.

Crosby is an uncompromising figure. I met him in 2010 at the Sky election debate in Bristol. Crosby was then out in the cold, with the Tories not using his services.

'Lynton had been snubbed by Steve Hilton and Andy Coulson,' says a senior Tory adviser.

With Cameron and Osborne, there were four people running the 2010 campaign. Hence, the disarray and chaos. Very arguably, they blew their advantage as a result of not having Lynton, or a Lynton – i.e. an experienced, disciplined, unafraid ringmaster. It meant they missed a majority and ultimately led to the referendum fiasco.

I was introduced to Crosby by a mutual friend at the bar in the hotel where the debates were being held.

'Is he a good guy?' Crosby said to my friend, barely acknowledging my presence.

'He certainly is, Lynton,' said my friend, a senior political adviser to the Tories.

With that, Crosby instantly warmed up, morphing immediately into a fount of political gossip and insider wisdom.

For the referendum campaign, he worked for neither side, but he did do a polling column in the *Daily Telegraph*.

On 30 May, Crosby wrote in the *Telegraph*, 'The Leave campaign increasing focus on lack of control over immigration and associated message discipline has helped their case.'

On 20 June, he said, 'The side that is most effective in motivating their voters to turn out on the 23rd will be the side that emerges victorious ... Only 4 per cent of the electorate is now undecided.'

Farage thinks the Tories should have paid greater heed to their old guru.

'They didn't listen [to Crosby in the *Telegraph*],' said Farage. 'He read the black days in the Out campaign very well and it was very much in response to that that the following Tuesday they came up with their Australian-style points system. Leave did listen to Crosby; Remain didn't.'

On 31 May, Boris Johnson and Michael Gove backed an Australian-style points system for potential immigrants, where points are awarded depending on age (you have to be under fifty to move to Australia), professional experience, qualifications and English language ability.

'Thank God, the snobs in the end got it,' says Farage. 'The day I saw Boris and Gove talk about the Australian-style points system, I nearly hit the ceiling I was so pleased. I knew we'd win.'

UKIP had the advantage of having the whole right-wing arena to themselves. There was no extremist party to force the debate further to the right.

'We were blessed with the demise of the BNP, who weren't there any more,' says Farage. 'I don't know what we would have done then.'

Some say UKIP were the dog-whistle party, sending out subtle racist signals to appeal to people who didn't like immigration. Farage denies the racist accusations. But, when it comes to immigration, Farage is happy to admit that the issue was front and centre of his campaign. On immigration, it wasn't a dog whistle that UKIP used: it was a huge klaxon, squawking out the anti-immigration message as its number one policy.

That message played well in the big cities of the north and the Midlands. On 31 May – the same day Johnson and Gove came out for an Australian-style points system – Farage went round the Rag Market in Birmingham. He was heckled by a Labour campaigner, Luke Holland, for his attendance record in the European Parliament, his MEP's salary and for 'blaming immigrants' for bankers' mistakes. But, elsewhere in the market, he was greeted warmly.

'The best bit of the campaign was the Rag Market in Birmingham,' says Farage.

That was stunning. It opens at 4 a.m., wholesale, fish, meat, vegetables. Then, from 9, it's retail. The men and women running these companies are hard-working, entrepreneurial people. In terms of religion and race, they were quite representative of Birmingham and yet the support in there was just unbelievable. They're working, running companies, living with the hygiene regulations that come from Brussels. That was a big moment.

That anti-immigration message was at its most controversial on 16 June 2016 – the day Nigel Farage released the most shocking poster of the campaign; the day the Labour MP Jo Cox was brutally murdered.

CHAPTER 8

16 JUNE:
THE MURDER OF JO COX

On 16 June, a week before the vote, the Brexiteers were relatively confident.

They had been lifted by the Battle of the Thames on 15 June – when a boat commanded by Bob Geldof stormed a flotilla of fishing boats led by Nigel Farage.

'The thing I'll remember most was the Battle of the Thames,' says Farage. Farage knew it played beautifully into his hands when a multi-millionaire Irish pop singer made abusive hand gestures at him from the poop deck of a pleasure boat.

'"Oh, thank you," I thought,' Farage says.

I had to ignore it all. He attacked me – fine. But, in the eyes of the fishing industry, I'd put the show on for them. That wasn't very clever. The biggest mistake was to say to them, 'What are you moaning about? You've got a great deal on the fish.' My son worked on a netter on the English Channel this summer.

Fucking hell, those boys work hard. You're up at four in the morning.

I shall never forget that [day on the Thames]. I had it on reliable information that the Essex contingent cracked the first can of something at about 5.30 that morning.

On that morning, then, the Leave camp were buoyant.

'Up until the day before the vote, I thought we were in with a very good chance,' says Farage.

The day of the Battle of the Thames that Thursday morning, I just thought we'd walked it. In fact, I was drinking champagne with quite a well-known public figure that lunchtime, who you wouldn't associate with our campaign. He said, 'I'm buying a bottle of fizz. You've done it.'

Then of course we had the Jo Cox murder. It didn't ultimately change a single vote. What it did do was take the big M out of our campaign – momentum. Did we get it back? A little bit. From the Tuesday onwards, we got a little bit back.

On the afternoon of 16 June, a week before the referendum, the Labour MP Jo Cox was shot dead in Birstall, West Yorkshire.

'Boris and Michael were very worried about the murder,' says Dominic Cummings. 'They were both upset. Gisela [Stuart] knew the poor lady and was upset on a very personal level: "I know her, I've met her kids."

'It was a personal shock to Michael and Gisela. I don't think Boris had met her.'

That morning also marked the most controversial moment of their campaign – the release of the poster showing a group of Syrians on the Slovenian border with the slogan 'Breaking point: the EU has failed us all'.

Farage remains unapologetic.

'The poster probably won it for us,' he says, before adding that he's being 'a bit tongue in cheek'.

'Had Jo Cox not been shot, you wouldn't have known anything about it. I launched a very similar poster in the first week in May, which should be criticised more because it was a mock-up: of London, with a two-mile queue coming into the city,' says Farage.

UKIP had paid for full-page adverts in national newspapers that morning, with that same Breaking Point image.

'It was a photograph,' he says.

What was the picture? It was aggressive young males, not refugees, trying to get into Europe, responding to the madness of Merkel, and the slogan 'The EU has failed us all'.

From midnight the night before, that was out and it was everywhere. We had full pages in the paper; poster trucks across the country. The only reason it got criticised was because the Remain camp said, 'This is it' [i.e. UKIP had gone too far].

Not everyone in UKIP agreed that the poster had been a good idea.

'I don't think that poster won us any votes at all,' says Douglas Carswell.

If that nativist message appealed to you, how are you going to vote anyway? The idea there was a two-tone campaign [with Farage appealing to one hard-right constituency and Vote Leave to a centrist one] is absolute tosh.

I won two elections for UKIP, and I mentioned immigration once, to say I wasn't anti individual immigrants. That nativist tone puts people off.

Dominic Cummings is also critical of the poster – and more broadly of Farage.

'Yes, Farage would motivate some non-voters,' says Cummings,

but there's another set of middle-class voters who don't like the EU and would have voted for us but didn't because they don't like Farage.

That was particularly the case after the murder and the poster. A bunch of middle-class people said, 'The EU is shit, but there's a good team and a bad team and, if I've got to choose, I'm not on his side. He's a wanker, I've got gay friends, black friends.'

Cummings conducted several focus groups on Farage and the poster in the last fortnight before the referendum.

'Overall, he was a negative,' says Cummings.

A lot of people were saying, 'I want to vote leave, but Farage, with that fucking stupid poster, we don't want to vote for that.'

Because of the murder, people saw that poster, and it made an unknown number queasy. Some still voted for us; some didn't. When the referendum came, a few million people thought, 'The EU's shit, but I am not on Farage's side,' and they voted in.

You don't need to do the poster. Who's that persuading? What good does that do? There's no empirical basis for saying it galvanises people. There's a strong basis for saying those it appealed to would vote anyway. But there was evidence that a whole lot of people would say, 'I'm not on that side.' Particularly with the context of that murder.

Although the received wisdom at the time was that Jo Cox's murder adversely affected the Leave side, both sides were nervous the following weekend, the last before the referendum.

David Cameron spent what was to be his last weekend as Prime Minister at Chequers, with his family and friends. He is said to have been very nervous, thinking he had lost.

'George Osborne was nervous from a few weeks before the referendum,' says one of the former Chancellor's senior advisers.

He had always felt more certain about the 2015 general election, where he was sure they'd got the message right. Even when the referendum polls were in Remain's favour, he remained unsure; he had been scarred by memories of the 1997 election, when some senior Tories had confidently predicted that this young man [Tony Blair] could never win.

And so, when private polls suggested Remain might win, Osborne thought they might squeak it – but he was never confident.

On Wednesday 22 June, Farage gave his final big speech at a Westminster conference centre.

'My last-minute appeal on the Wednesday morning was completely designed to go out all points west: if you've never voted in your life, this is the one time,' he says.

In the end, the murder of Jo Cox – for all its extreme horror, and the disgust it provoked – appears to have had little effect on the result of the referendum.

'When the polls moved towards us before the murder, the physicists said, "You're going to win,"' says Dominic Cummings.

The polls moved away afterwards – but you couldn't be sure if the pollsters were tweaking the methodology. The assumption in London was that this was good for the In campaign. It's logical.

We weren't pessimistic about the result the way others were. I said, 'Look at the averages.' In some, we're behind; in some, we're ahead. On the ten-day rolling averages, it's about 50–50.

The day after the murder, on 17 June, Henry de Zoete, a former adviser to Michael Gove in the Department for Education, conducted focus groups for Vote Leave about how Jo Cox's murder would affect the referendum result.

'People didn't understand the question,' says Dominic Cummings.

'How would it affect my vote? A nutter. What's that got to do with the referendum?' Henry came back and said, 'We're still alive.'

The polls bounced around. They trended against us – but you couldn't tell if it was tweaked. They all tweaked things in the last few days. I'm still worried about turnout. The murder might motivate a lot of young people.

The murder of Jo Cox led to a three-day suspension of campaigning.

'I remember Nigel and I worrying whether the momentum has gone,' says Chris Bruni-Lowe. 'But I think people had already made their mind up. If you look at Lynton Crosby's polling, in the main, and how many undecided would change their mind, the answer was very few.'

When the moratorium was lifted, Farage was in the eye of the storm.

'It gave me in political terms probably the toughest couple of days that I'd ever had, on the Sunday and the Monday – Osborne saying I'd driven things back to Nazi Germany and unbelievable stuff,' Farage says. 'They really went for it and I didn't give an inch. Gove said it had appalled them, although look at the stuff they were running online on Abu Hamza.'

Farage is referring to online literature from Vote Leave

saying that, because of the EU, Britain was constrained from removing terrorist sympathisers.

'As demonstrated by the Government's flagging attempts to deport Chaymae Smak,' said the literature. 'Smak, a Moroccan national, was convicted of conveying a SIM card into prison for her father-in-law, convicted terrorist Abu Hamza al-Masri.'

Farage thinks the firestorm over the poster was crucial in putting immigration at the top of the agenda.

'We got together here on the Tuesday morning,' Farage says, referring to UKIP's Westminster HQ.

It was rough – death threats coming through every five minutes. We sat here and they were talking immigration.

Suddenly, I was being called off to studios all over London not to talk about the poster directly, but to talk about immigration, and the debate was back on. And we got the momentum going again.

Jacob Rees-Mogg was the only one of the Tories who said, well, ironically, the poster and the furore got the debate back to where it needed to be. Was that planned? No.

There is an alternative theory that the three-day moratorium on campaigning actually harmed the Remain campaign.

'There's a different perspective, which isn't necessarily correct – that Cameron and Osborne had a massive barrage lined up with Carney, [for] the day after the murder,' says Dominic Cummings. 'There is a plausible argument that they screwed themselves, thinking, "All good, right-thinking people must vote against Out." They lose focus and fuck up. Matthew Hancock [pro-EU Tory MP for Portsmouth] spent the next week tweeting broken-heart symbols.

'Arguably, it helped us. Instead of having Carney and Project Fear, they got emotional.'

On the day of the referendum, the truth was that – as is so often the case in politics, and life – no one knew what was going to happen.

CHAPTER 9

REFERENDUM DAY:
NO ONE KNOWS ANYTHING

At different times on the day of the referendum, both sides thought they'd won – and lost.

The only person who was really confident about a Leave victory was Nigel Farage's chauffeur – who bet £1,000 on Leave and won £6,000.

'I went up and down,' says Daniel Hannan. 'In my lower moments in the campaign, I thought there was only a 40 per cent chance of victory.'

'I was nervous through the entire campaign about the result,' says Nigel Farage. 'The only time I lost my nerve was at lunchtime on polling day – eleventh-hour nerves – after I saw what the markets did in the morning.'

That was when the pound soared, because City investors, using private polling, thought Remain had won.

'Having worked in the markets, I know they can be cretinous, but that cretinous?' says Nigel Farage. 'I also said to people on that day, "Fairy tales never come true." Because for me it's like a fairy tale.'

In fact, the City pollsters had got their polling wrong. What had happened was that Eurosceptics tended to go out early to vote. 'Because they're the most passionate in wanting to leave,' says Chris Bruni-Lowe. The City pollsters had factored this into their calculations, because they expected a big Europhile vote to turn out in the afternoon – which never materialised.

After the pound soared in the morning when Remain were in the ascendant, it dropped in the afternoon – thanks, it's thought, to huge bets made on Brexit by hedge funders, who had done their own private polling, and seen that Leave was ahead. The hedge funder Crispin Odey is said to have made £220 million out of the Brexit vote.

'The conventional view was that, by the evening, Remainers would vote on their way home from work,' says Chris Bruni-Lowe. 'It started to rain really heavily that day, particularly in London. And the Remain side weren't as passionate in turning out.'

Still, no one could be sure of the result when polls closed at 10 p.m. Nigel Farage, now at Chris Bruni-Lowe's house in Westminster, had a wobble at 10.03 p.m. Shaving upstairs, he said to a Sky News interviewer over the phone, 'Remain will edge it.'

'We were totally surprised when Nigel semi-conceded,' said Chris Bruni-Lowe. 'He said, "I'm going upstairs to shave." In the meantime, he talked to someone from Sky News, saying, "I think we've lost this." We've no idea why.'

In fact, Leavers as a whole weren't optimistic about winning. That afternoon, at 12.05 p.m., the pollster Peter Kellner of YouGov predicted a Remain win by 8.5 per cent. At 9 p.m., David Cameron's pollster, Andrew Cooper, was predicting a 53–47 win for Remain. In Downing Street, where David Cameron was holding a small party for friends and close advisers, the mood was buoyant.

'Farage thought we were going to lose all the way through,' says Dominic Cummings.

> The YouGov exit poll, 52 to 48 for In, came out at 10. It confirmed his worst fears. He'd been thinking about how he conducts himself after the vote.
>
> Michael [Gove] went to bed, thinking we'd lost. He went to bed at 10. On the day of the referendum, I was 50–50. Before the murder of Jo Cox, I think we're going to win. After, I don't know. I thought different things at different points in the day.

At the Vote Leave HQ on the south bank of the Thames, the physicists were still tapping away on their laptops through the day, examining their models and comparing their expectations to news coming in from the ground. They also had in front of them the BBC's polling expectations, and those by the polling expert Professor John Curtice of Strathclyde University.

In addition, they had a list of figures for each count which would equate with a 50–50 nationwide poll; any variation in those figures, one way or the other, predicted a win or a lose vote.

'From the very first numbers that come in, they type in the information,' says Cummings. 'They say, "That's good... that's good." From the very beginning, it seems the numbers on the ground were positive.'

All through the day, people in counting stations were tweeting and texting observations from the polling stations. After the polls closed, when the ballot boxes were unloaded, tellers started putting the votes into piles. Before any official tallies were done, you could already get a rough idea of what's happening.

'Within the first hour already, the physicists said, if these numbers are accurate, you're going to win,' says Cummings. 'Shit, we might have actually won this thing.'

The first concrete sign that Leave might have won came with the Sunderland result – 61.3 per cent out to 38.7 per cent in.

'Sunderland was a big moment but we didn't absolutely know,' says Nigel Farage.

Over at Vote Leave, the confidence was building, too.

'Pretty much they're coming in – yup, that's good for us,' says Dominic Cummings. 'Gradually, the momentum starts to build. There's a massive deafening roar going up in the office as Robert Peston starts putting up charts predicting a win.'

Douglas Carswell was a guest on the BBC as the results came in. He had brought with him a document showing what the result should be in each region, if the overall vote was going to be 50–50.

'I was on air with Dimbleby and Amber Rudd when Sunderland and Newcastle came in,' says Carswell. 'My paper for 50–50 in Sunderland said 53 per cent; it was 61 per cent. I turned round to Dimbleby when we weren't broadcasting and said, "This is amazing."'

When the Birmingham result came in – Leave won 50.4 per cent of the vote – they had all but won.

Birmingham has talismanic value today for Leavers.

'The time I spent in Birmingham in a solidly Labour area was instructive – the enthusiasm of people who weren't normally enthused by politics,' says Douglas Carswell. 'People in Birmingham would talk about "they" – and they saw it as a vote against them [MPs], also against the people who read out the news.'

Nigel Farage went from Chris Bruni-Lowe's house, off Horseferry Road in Westminster, to the Leave.EU party in the Sky Bar in Millbank Tower – which is kitted out like a New York loft, with bare brick walls, and has a wraparound view of the Thames and the London skyline.

'When we absolutely knew, we tried to get a gigantic bet on,' says Farage. 'It was half past three in the morning; we were downwind of a few. All the bookies were awake but I couldn't get a bean on. Well, nothing sensible.'

It was Bruni-Lowe who tried to put on that huge sum at three in the morning. 'No one would take the money,' he says.

Over at Downing Street, the mood had collapsed. Friends

of the Camerons left the party in the small hours, knowing all was lost.

'It was like leaving a party after the host's had a row or something,' says a friend of the Camerons who was there. 'Do you say goodbye or do you just sneak out? I left the room with a muted goodbye at the door.'

At 3 a.m. on 24 June, Cameron was in his No. 10 study with his close advisers. Knowing the game was up, he quoted the old Enoch Powell line, 'All political lives end in failure.'

'At 4 a.m., I made the speech: a new dawn is breaking,' says Nigel Farage.

When I heard that the leaders of Vote Leave were asleep, I realised this didn't mean much to them in quite the way it did to me.

I kept saying, 'Is this really happening?' or 'What's in that glass?' It was an amazing feeling. We were all here [in UKIP's Westminster HQ], mob-handed. We went to a London hotel for champagne and kippers – it seemed the appropriate thing to do. I kept going, all through the night, all through the day until three the next morning. I worked in the City in the 1980s. We're used to working through the night.

With Michael Gove in bed and Boris Johnson lying doggo, that left Nigel Farage to claim public victory with his Independence Day speech, declaring, 'Dawn is breaking on an independent United Kingdom.' 23 June, he said, should go down as 'Independence Day'.

Over at Vote Leave HQ on the south bank of the Thames
– just across the river from the Leave.EU party in Millbank
Tower – a group of around fifty Vote Leavers, Bernard Jenkin
among them, had also realised they had won. The physicists
had declared they were almost certain of a Brexit vote, just
before the broadcasters confirmed it. They wanted to wait for
the turnout data for London before they were 95 per cent sure.

At this point, Daniel Hannan got up in the Vote Leave HQ
and gave a victory speech. Hannan, a Shakespeare aficio-
nado, channelled Henry V's St Crispin's Day speech on the
eve of Agincourt, inserting the names of leading Vote Leave
campaigners:

> We few, we happy few, we band of brothers;
> For he to-day that sheds his blood with me
> Shall be my brother; be he ne'er so vile,
> This day shall gentle his condition;
> And gentlemen in England now a-bed
> Shall think themselves accurs'd they were not here,
> And hold their manhoods cheap whiles any speaks
> That fought with us upon Saint Crispin's day.

Dominic Cummings was in a different room, down the corridor, still processing results with the physicists.

At 4.40 a.m., David Dimbleby said, on the BBC, 'And the
answer is: we're out.'

At that moment, as Hannan was finishing his speech, the
Vote Leave workers started chanting, 'Dom, Dom, Dom...'

Hearing this, Cummings left the small room and joined the crowd in the main room, overlooking Parliament and the Thames.

'Dan said something very nice and gracious,' says Cummings. 'I got up on the table and said, "You guys did this, well done."'

Cummings stood on the table, slightly crouching to avoid bumping his head on the plasterboard ceiling above. He asked the audience twice why they had asked people to vote Leave. Twice, they shouted, 'Take back control.'

In a rare moment of emotion, Cummings punched the air and, in the process, accidentally whacked the ceiling with his fist, dislodging the plasterboard panel above his head.

Lambeth Bridge, which connects the south bank of the Thames – and the home of the Vote Leave offices – to the Palace of Westminster, was unusually busy on the morning of 24 June 2016.

At 5 a.m., Douglas Carswell was walking across the bridge towards Westminster, when he began channelling William Wordsworth, who had mused on a similar early morning view from neighbouring Westminster Bridge in 1802.

'I stopped,' Carswell says.

I could see the Archbishop of Canterbury's Palace at Lambeth, Westminster, the BBC on Millbank, with Downing Street beyond, and I thought, we've just beaten the whole bloody lot of you. Bishops, mandarins, ministers, they were almost all on the other side. If you take your cue as to what is normal from those grandees, you're going to be a little disorientated.

If he'd waited on the bridge for a while longer, Carswell would have bumped into Charles Moore, the *Daily Telegraph* columnist and the paper's former editor, walking in the opposite direction.

'As I crossed Lambeth Bridge at 6 a.m., groups of youthful, revelling Leavers coming the other way recognised me and came up and kissed me,' said Moore.

By this stage, Farage had called for David Cameron to stand down that day, which he duly did at 8 a.m.

'On a human level, despite everything, I did feel a bit sorry for David that next morning,' says Farage. 'He's not a bad bloke, who just happened to be at the wrong point in time in history.'

And does he feel sorry for George Osborne?

'I personally would like to see Osborne openly tarred and feathered,' he says. 'I hope he never shows his pasty face again in public.'

But who would fill the Cameron–Osborne vacuum? The bloody fight for the crown had begun: the king is dead; long live the king. And, at that early stage, the leading contender for the throne was obvious – Boris Johnson.

CHAPTER 10

COMETH THE HOUR,
COMETH THE BLOND:
BORIS'S MOMENT
IN THE SUN

In 2006, Boris Johnson said of the Tory Party that it had 'become used to Papua New Guinea-style orgies of cannibalism and chief-killing'.

Shortly afterwards, he said, 'I mean no insult to the people of Papua New Guinea, who I'm sure lead lives of blameless bourgeois domesticity in common with the rest of us ... Add Papua New Guinea to my global itinerary of apologies.'

In fact, Boris had underplayed the rabid lust for blood felt by Tories in search of new leaders. In the three weeks after the Brexit vote, when the Conservative candidates were jockeying for position, you could smell the napalm in the air, morning, noon and night. Theresa May, Andrea Leadsom, Michael Gove, Stephen Crabb and Liam Fox were sucked into a vortex of mutual destruction so powerful that the favourite, Boris Johnson, was jettisoned from the race even before he declared his formal intention to stand.

If you wanted a little taste of brimstone in those short, crazed weeks, all you had to do was ring an adviser to a Tory candidate. A close confidant of Boris's told me he wanted to kneecap Dominic Cummings, Michael Gove's right-hand man, shortly after Boris was stabbed in the back by Gove – even though it is said by insiders that Cummings had nothing to do with the knifing and left the fray after the referendum victory.

'If we're not careful,' Boris's confidant told me, just before Theresa May became Prime Minister, 'we're going to end up with Gove on the steps of No. 10, with Lady Macbeth [Sarah Vine, Gove's wife] on one side, and fucking Rasputin [Dominic Cummings] on the other.'

After Boris was knifed, another of his senior advisers had a series of commemorative coasters made – they showed Michael Gove, mid-speech, in the same colours and font as the Barack Obama 'Hope' poster. The slogan on the Gove one was 'NOPE'.

Over those three weeks between the referendum and Theresa May's coronation, the British body politic underwent a mammoth nervous breakdown. Not only was there the mass political murder that sent Bullingdon blood sluicing down Downing Street. There was mass political suicide, too, as two thirds of Labour's shadow Cabinet resigned in protest at Jeremy Corbyn's colossal incompetence, and Nigel Farage removed himself – if only temporarily – from the fray. The survivors were left paralysed – as they, like the honourable members of the British press, had absolutely no idea what was going to happen.

A nervous fever spread across the country. On the evening of Friday 24 June, I had a drink in the Red Lion in Duke of York Street in St James's, London. Walking back from the bar to my friend, I passed four different groups of people – of different ages and backgrounds – and all of them were talking about Brexit. The British don't usually like talking seriously, or at length, about politics – now they could talk of nothing else.

In this febrile, blood-soaked atmosphere, everyone blamed each other.

At the *Spectator* party in the garden of their Westminster office on 6 July, less than a fortnight after the referendum, a Tory peer, appointed by David Cameron, proceeded to lay into him.

'David Cameron's a cunt,' he said, boosted by several pints of *The Spectator*'s Pol Roger. 'He got us in this mess and he did absolutely fuck all to get us out of it.'

None of the walking dead of the Tory Party turned up to that event – no Boris, no Cameron, no Osborne; all of them usually regular attenders. One contender was there – Theresa May – but she barely sent a ripple through the crowd of politics addicts in *The Spectator*'s jam-packed garden. Little did they suspect that, just a week later, she would become Prime Minister.

The real, quivering, close-to-violence anger came from Boris Johnson's camp after Michael Gove's last-minute

– more like last-second – switcheroo. Boris was poleaxed by Gove's treachery, not least because they had so recently been friends and allies on the campaign trail. In one old speech praising the then Education Secretary, Boris said of Gove that 'he gove us free schools; he gove us freedom from government control of schools'.

Ever since Michael Gove turned Brutus to his Caesar, Boris must use 'gove' in a quite different sense. Johnson the classical scholar knows Caesar's last words weren't the Latin, '*Et tu, Brute?*' They were the more affectionate Greek: '*Kai su, teknon?*' – 'You too, my child?'

That's how Boris felt after he had been axed by Gove – like he'd been betrayed by his nearest and dearest. Friends said he was particularly upset by the idea that he lost his nerve when he dropped out of the race just when he was supposed to be announcing his leadership bid.

And they could so easily have done it together, with Boris as PM, Gove as Chancellor of the Exchequer.

'If Michael hadn't done what he'd done, the two of them would have been in charge of the country – Boris would have won,' says Dominic Cummings.

Boris would almost certainly have made it to the final round of voting, in which one of two MPs is chosen by the largely Eurosceptic, largely Borisophile members. The Johnson–Gove coronation was a racing certainty – but for Gove's volte-face.

And that double coronation had been planned some time before the referendum.

'A month before the vote, Michael is in a bit of a state,' says Dominic Cummings. 'He says, "I think we're going to win. David and George are finished. The grown-ups are all going to get kicked out. Everyone's going to say, 'You've got to stand as leader against Boris,' and I don't want to do it."'

Cummings agreed that Cameron and Osborne were finished if there was a Leave vote.

'You're right, but you don't have to stand against Boris,' Cummings said to Gove. 'No one can force you to do anything you don't want to do. Chill out.'

A week later, Boris, too, was beginning to realise that Leave might win – and what that might mean for him.

Cummings says:

For the first time, Boris says to me, 'We might bloody win this thing, you know. I think I should probably go for it. What does the Gover think? Is the Gover going to go for it? If the Gover's running, maybe I should support him. But will that work? What do you think?'

Cummings said, 'Michael doesn't want to do it. He shouldn't do it. You two should do a deal. My feeling is that it's very unpleasant, you two winning and then fighting about who's leader afterwards.'

Never was a truer word spoken.

'You should do a deal,' Cummings told Boris. 'I've always thought Michael shouldn't be leader.'

'What sort of deal?' Boris asked.

'Make Michael Chancellor and in charge of civil service reform.'

'Why civil service reform?' asked Boris.

'Because it's the hardest thing since beating the Nazis that the British state has had to do. And you have to do it with a fucked-up system. Everyone will tell you you can't do two massive things at the same time. You can only do Brexit properly if you change how the system works and get great people in. Churchill in the war didn't just accept how the system worked. He went in and shifted it around.'

'Yes,' said Boris, 'the Gover knows how to do this. You've done all this before in the DFE [Department for Education].'

It was all a perfectly friendly chat. Johnson and Cummings referred to it again a couple more times before the referendum. The only time the leadership question came up again in earnest was on the evening of 16 June – the day Jo Cox was killed. A dinner – planned before the murder – was held, at which a group of Gove's friends and advisers met to discuss the leadership at the request of Sarah Vine, Gove's wife.

One senior Tory at the dinner said, 'You should go for it.'

Dominic Cummings recalls, 'Me and Zoete [Henry de Zoete, a Gove adviser] said, "No, do a deal with Boris." At the end, Michael said, "It was a good discussion, thanks very much. I agree with Henry and Dominic. I'm not going to do it." It was categorical and clear.'

No deal was seriously considered until the Sunday before the vote – 19 June – when Cummings and Gove met Johnson at Boris's house in Islington.

Cummings suggested meeting Gove at a pub round the corner beforehand.

'Are you happy to do a deal with Boris?' Cummings asked Gove. 'Here's the deal. You're Chancellor and you're also dealing with civil service reform. Are you happy with it? Now's the moment to say.'

'Absolutely. I'm happy with it,' Gove said.

'My view is maybe you'll be better at the job than him but my view is that you haven't got certain temperamental aspects needed to be PM,' said Cummings.

You're a very nice guy. But, in lots of ways, that's a bad thing. To be PM, you need an element of coldness and toughness, and to make decisions without being upset. I know you and, because you're a very nice guy, I'm worried you wouldn't be able to do it without pulling you and your family apart, torturing yourself over things, matters of life and death. It's totally different to what you've done before. It's possible you may be brilliant at it. But I don't think you would.

Boris has got flaws, but the best thing for the country is to do a deal. He's got a better chance psychologically of handling it, particularly if we do civil service reform. I can go off and bring in lots of people, rip up the civil service HR rules, rewire the way Downing Street works.

The civil service was also seen by some Eurosceptics as essentially Europhile.

'People say there was no plan [after the referendum],' says

Douglas Carswell. 'Vote Leave had thought through the public policy implications in great detail, that we can't entrust this to civil servants.'

Cummings's view was that Gove and Johnson may not have been the best-qualified people to run the country, but they were very far from being the worst. He thought there was a way of building the system around them that would take advantage of their good points and deal with their bad points.

'Michael said, "I agree with you – we should do a deal,"' says Cummings.

With this settled, they walked round the corner to Boris's house.

'Boris said to Michael, "Are you going to do it?"' says Cummings. 'Michael said, "I haven't 100 per cent decided. I have 99.9 per cent decided and I want to support you."'

That 0.1 per cent would have something to say for itself a few weeks later. But, for now, Gove and Johnson were as one.

'Boris said, in a roundabout way, "What do you want?"' says Cummings. 'Michael said, "It's up to you if you're PM. But I've thought a lot about this sort of thing and Dominic and I have thought a lot about the way the government works. That's [i.e. civil service reform] what I'd like to do."'

'Boris said, "That's very sensible."'

Cummings had promised his wife, Mary Wakefield, that he would leave the political stage after the referendum, win or lose. If the Johnson–Gove team got into Downing Street, then he would consider a job – but, otherwise, he was off.

What about the suggestion, made by Nigel Farage, that Cummings was pushing for Gove as Prime Minister, with him as chief of staff?

'That's 100 per cent untrue,' says Cummings.

I spoke to Michael several times and he said, without exception, 'I don't want to do this and I'm not going to do it.'

There was never at any point any sort of plan for Michael being PM. The only discussions were about how to make Boris Prime Minister. Boris knows it's untrue because of my conversations about it with him.

The meeting continued with lots of conversations about the mechanics of a leadership bid – what to do with cameras, paparazzi, the inevitable chaos and where their children could be safely based.

'Essentially, it's all agreed,' says Cummings.

After this meeting, Gove and Johnson returned to the referendum campaign, with the skeleton of their leadership bid settled.

The leadership question came back to the fore on the morning of Friday 24 June, the day after the referendum. That morning, Boris came into the Vote Leave office on the South Bank and met Cummings in a little room off the corridor.

'Boris says, "Where are we on this?"' says Cummings.

In between discussing the leadership bid, Boris showed his delight at the referendum result.

'It's fucking brilliant,' he says. 'We fucking did it.'

Gove soon joined Johnson in the little room to have a discussion about the leadership.

'They emerge after half an hour, all smiles,' says Cummings. 'Everyone happy. Yes, agreed, we know what we're doing.'

Johnson and Gove then went to give their joint press conference – where they both looked stunned and miserable.

'Some people say that slight dazed look in Boris and Michael's eyes was indicative that they hadn't been authentic,' says Douglas Carswell.

In fact, it shows how authentic they'd been – they'd risked their careers for it, they hadn't done it for steps one, two, three and four [in their careers].

The fact that Boris and Michael didn't have a scheme for what happened next showed they were authentic. If they wanted to take over as leader, they might have worked out what to do next.

The events of that week are so crowded and complicated that it's best to tell the story as what Rachel Johnson calls 'a tick-tock' – a blow-by-blow account of the whole gripping saga.

The Johnson leadership bid began in earnest on the Saturday morning, 25 June.

'There was a phone call between Boris and Gove,' said a senior member of Boris's campaign team. 'Gove wanted to be Chancellor, Deputy Prime Minister and chief Brexit negotiator. Boris agreed only on Chancellor.'

Gove remained in London and had a meeting with Cummings and two other advisers in Cummings's house in Islington. They discussed more details about the Johnson–Gove deal. Gove and an adviser suggested to Mary Wakefield, Cummings's wife, that she should let Cummings work in Downing Street.

At the same time, Boris set off for a game of cricket at Althorp House, Northamptonshire, home of Earl Spencer – Princess Diana's brother and Boris's old Eton and Oxford contemporary. The match was between Lord Spencer's XI and a Johnson XI.

And it was Boris's hubris – in playing cricket that weekend and, later that week, allegedly not finishing his leadership speech on time – that partly led to his downfall.

This display of pleasure over business was the first blow to Gove–Johnson relations – Gove was said to have been alarmed on hearing about the cricket match. Throughout the referendum campaign, Gove had worked happily alongside Boris – under the direction of Vote Leave. After the referendum, Gove was de facto working for Boris – and he found Boris's unreliability a nightmare.

I well know from working with Boris at the *Telegraph* that prompt timekeeping is not his forte. For five years, my Wednesday nights were destroyed as Boris regularly missed the 7 p.m. deadline for delivering his column. 'It hasn't arrived,' I'd say to him over the phone at 7.01 p.m.

'Ah, Christ, sorry,' said Boris. 'Bloody internet! It must be pinging its way down those threadbare copper wires as we speak, old man.'

In fact, he hadn't finished writing the column. I could hear him tapping away at his keyboard on the other end of the phone, while insisting he'd already sent it.

The lateness wasn't because he was lazy. One of Boris's brilliant ruses is to give the impression of idle chaos, in order to disguise the diamond-hard ambition that lurks beneath. He gets up at 5.45 a.m. every day. And on those Wednesday evenings, he had already put *The Spectator* to bed, been to Prime Minister's Questions and perhaps written his *GQ* car column.

And yet he was vilified for his supposed laziness – for captaining a team of Johnsons against Lord Spencer's XI at Althorp.

Boris is, in fact, a Stakhanovite worker, who squeezes bursts of pleasure – of all sorts – in between much longer stretches of activity. One of his sayings is, 'I have no time to write – so I write in no time.'

The fact that he wrote those two alternative *Telegraph* columns before he came out for Leave in February 2016 speaks volumes. He normally didn't have the time to write one; to write two shows that he was in a real, desperate quandary about the issue – thus his rare classical mistake in his pro-Europe column.

Boris is in the unusual position of being intensely ambitious while, at the same time, understanding the laughable nature of ambition.

'Though he sincerely wants power – because he must win – he knows that all political ambition is absurd,' says Stuart Reid, his deputy editor at *The Spectator*. 'He knows, too, that politics is absurd. The result is that, when he makes a political pitch, there is always an element of satire in his words and manner.'

Boris would also have liked the intense romance, and intense Englishness, of a game of cricket in the shadow of one of England's great country houses, in the company of its noble owner.

It's not that Boris is a snob – far from it. But he is seduced by the dash and history of the English upper classes.

'There's a part of Boris that is the European intellectual that likes a park, a big house and the aristocracy,' says an old schoolfriend. 'That element of aristocratic honour that meant he would defend Darius Guppy.'

The old schoolfriend is referring to the embarrassing occasion when Boris agreed to give Guppy – Boris's Eton, Oxford and Bullingdon friend – the address of a *News of the World* journalist Guppy wanted beaten up. Boris never actually gave him the address, and the journalist survived unscathed.

'Boris knows he is much more intelligent than his upper-class friends but he still likes the idea of them,' says the old schoolfriend.

To Boris, batting at Althorp while Britain was splitting itself down the middle was like Sir Francis Drake finishing his game of bowls as the Armada sailed over the horizon.

'It wasn't the most sensible thing to do,' says Dominic

Cummings. 'But it's not the disastrous, stupid thing it turned into, once everything's gone tits up. If Boris had won, everyone would have said, "What sangfroid, in the best tradition of the English…"'

By 7 p.m. on the evening of Saturday 25 June, the cricket match was over. Johnson, Gove and Cummings talked that evening. Cummings wrote down what they had all agreed, and emailed the conclusions to the other two.

'Boris and Michael both said, "Yes, that's what we both agreed – Michael as Chancellor, in charge of civil service reform, a few other personnel things,"' says Cummings.

They also concluded that Cummings wouldn't be involved with the leadership campaign. He might, though, get a job in Downing Street, depending on the wishes of his wife, Mary Wakefield. He says he was happy not to be involved if no one wanted him around.

The harmony in the Johnson–Gove team began to fray on Sunday 26 June, when Boris held a barbecue for supporters at his old constituency house in Oxfordshire. At the boozy barbecue, Gove got the impression Boris and his supporters weren't doing enough to prepare Boris's leadership campaign – which Gove had agreed to chair, while Lynton Crosby did the day-to-day campaigning.

'On the Sunday night, there were the first hints of discord,' says Dominic Cummings. 'Michael had just been off to this barbecue. It was chaos, with second-rate MPs suggesting that we announce Boris's leadership now, outside the barbecue, calling up people from the BBC and then cancelling it.'

Gove said to Cummings, 'I've got a very bad feeling about this.' He then asked Cummings to come over to dinner the following night.

Things got worse the next day, with the publication of Boris's regular Monday column in the *Daily Telegraph*. Gove is said to have seen, and made changes to, the column. But, still, that didn't stop the column coming across as distinctly lacking in red meat to hardcore Brexiteers.

'It is said that those who voted Leave were mainly driven by anxieties about immigration. I do not believe that is so,' wrote Boris.

> After meeting thousands of people in the course of the campaign, I can tell you that the number one issue was control – a sense that British democracy was being undermined by the EU system, and that we should restore to the people that vital power: to kick out their rulers at elections, and to choose new ones…
>
> The only change – and it will not come in any great rush – is that the UK will extricate itself from the EU's extraordinary and opaque system of legislation: the vast and growing corpus of law enacted by a European Court of Justice from which there can be no appeal. This will bring not threats, but golden opportunities for this country – to pass laws and set taxes according to the needs of the UK.

By this stage, Gove was beginning to worry about the Boris bid. At the beginning of that week – according to one account

– Gove and his fellow MP Nick Boles discussed how to bring Boris into line.

One insider compared it to the scene in *The Wind in the Willows* when Mole, Rat and Badger try to rein in Toad's addiction to fast cars: 'Cried the Mole delightedly, "Hooray! I remember now! We'll teach him to be a sensible Toad."'

They all then walk to Toad Hall, to find Toad in goggles, cap, gaiters and enormous overcoat. Rat proceeds to sit on him; Mole takes off his driving clothes. And then Badger reads Toad the riot act:

> 'You've disregarded all the warnings we've given you, you've gone on squandering the money your father left you, and you're getting us animals a bad name in the district by your furious driving and your smashes and your rows with the police.'
>
> 'That's no good!' said the Rat contemptuously. 'Talking to Toad'll never cure him. He'll say anything.'

Toad undertakes to Badger to give up cars altogether, only to rebel, shouting, 'I faithfully promise that the very first motor-car I see, poop-poop! Off I go in it.'

Even when they lock Toad in his bedroom, he escapes, and rushes off and steals a car from the car park of the Red Lion, only to be caught by the police and jailed for twenty years.

And so it was with Boris. He agreed with Gove and Boles not to do any furious driving, or any poop-pooping, only to let them down again over the following three days.

On the evening of Monday 27 June, Dominic Cummings went over to Michael Gove's house in north Kensington.

'He's a bit agitated, all a bit chaotic, with these clowns running around, no structure,' says Cummings.

Gove suggested that Cummings accompany him to a meeting with Lynton Crosby on the following morning.

'Boris says he's going to get a grip on everything – will you come along?' Gove asked Cummings. Cummings wasn't sure.

'Lynton might think I'm trying to muscle in,' Cummings said.

'I'd be happy if you did come along,' said Gove. 'Boris knows you.'

Cummings agreed to go to the breakfast the next morning in Crosby's office in Old Park Lane, in Mayfair, between Green Park and Hyde Park. After that meeting, Cummings said, he would be leaving on holiday.

Cummings, Gove, Johnson and Crosby were at the 8 a.m. meeting – along with a colleague of Crosby's, Mark Fullbrook, and Ben Wallace, the Conservative MP for Wyre and Preston North. Wallace was helping to run Boris's leadership bid.

'Things were quite honestly discussed,' says Cummings.

I said, 'I'm not there but everyone's saying Boris's office is a shambles, no one's in charge of anything, people wandering in and out. There's no grip, no one monitoring who says what.'

Ben Wallace says, 'It isn't true, don't believe any of those stories.'

Lynton says, 'It fucking is true, mate. That's exactly what's happened. You've fucked the whole thing up. And you're babbling on to the media as well.'

Ben Wallace looks very hangdog. Boris looks a bit embarrassed.

Lynton says, 'I've got some very good people. They'll be there by lunchtime. They're going to get a grip of all this stuff. There'll be someone on the door, diary people.'

With all this settled, Boris asked Cummings what his plans were. Cummings said he was off on holiday; that he wouldn't work on the leadership bid, but he would have a think about working in Downing Street.

'Boris said to Gove, in front of Lynton, "Everything's agreed, you're going to be Chancellor," says Cummings, who then prepared to leave on holiday.

Not everyone was happy with the meeting.

'When Gove walks in with Cummings, we could either say, "Fuck off," or we could grin and bear it. We went for the latter option,' said a senior member of Boris's campaign team. 'Gove acknowledged we had serious concerns about Cummings, but he assured us he'd play no role in the leadership campaign. Cummings said he was only involved in what would happen in No. 10.'

After that meeting, the Johnson–Gove team prepared a website and the campaign office.

Free for the first time in months, Cummings strolled round the corner from Crosby's office to have breakfast in Shepherd Market. While he was there, he got a phone call from Henry Cook, a Gove adviser, with some bad news. Sarah Vine, Michael Gove's wife, had sent an email to Gove and his special advisers with some strategy advice – which was then leaked to the press. Accidentally, she had sent the email to Tom Newman, a fashion PR, rather than Henry Newman, one of Gove's advisers.

The email read:

Very important that we focus on the individual obstacles and thoroughly overcome them before moving to the next. I really think Michael needs to have a Henry [Cook] or a Beth [Armstrong, another Gove special adviser] with him for this morning's crucial meetings.

One simple message: you MUST have SPECIFIC assurances from Boris OTHERWISE you cannot guarantee your support. The details can be worked out later on, but without that you have no leverage.

Crucially, the membership will not have the necessary re-assurance to back Boris, neither will [*Daily Mail* editor Paul] Dacre/[head of News Corporation, Rupert] Murdoch, who instinctively dislike Boris but trust your ability enough to support a Boris Gove ticket.

Do not concede any ground. Be your stubborn best.
GOOD LUCK.

Some commentators suggest the email was leaked on purpose. It seems unlikely – the email, when publicised, brought no obvious advantage to Team Gove. Still, it was the first public sign that all was not harmonious between Gove and Johnson. Things were about to get a whole lot less harmonious.

'It was almost the ultimate example that it's cock-up not conspiracy,' says Cummings. 'Henry said, "What do we do?" I said, "Don't worry about it."'

The following morning, Wednesday 29 June, at another Johnson campaign meeting, Gove referred to the email.

Vine maintains she accidentally sent the email to the wrong recipient, but Boris's camp claim she leaked it, to undermine Boris's chances. Vine had also allegedly tipped off the BBC that Leave campaigners were meeting at Boris's Oxfordshire home the previous Sunday.

'Gove said, "Sarah's sent an email to the wrong person," and he effectively laughed it off,' said the Team Boris member. 'Someone said, "I hope she won't write anything else." And Gove said, "Of course she will – that's her job." He should have said, "Don't worry, I'll sort it out." Of course, the email was leaked on purpose.'

In those fevered days of mass leaking, both teams went into overdrive, trying to quash the rumours put about by their opponents.

'Of course the email wasn't leaked [by Vine],' a member of Gove's inner circle told me. 'Why on earth would she want to name Paul Dacre in the email – her boss at the *Mail*?'

Leaking was a problem with Gove himself, too, according to Ben Wallace MP, Boris's campaign manager, who said,

'Michael seems to have an emotional need to gossip, particularly when drink is taken, as it all too often seemed to be.'

At that same Wednesday morning meeting, campaign roles were apportioned. Gove became Boris's campaign chairman. Nick Boles, an MP and Gove's former flatmate, ran the MPs' nomination process. Dominic Raab MP managed Brexit strategy. Beth Armstrong, a Gove adviser, controlled the master list of Tory MPs who might back Johnson in the ballot.

'That list is the Holy Grail,' said a senior member of Boris's campaign team.

> They had taken away the ability from Boris to operate without Gove's people. He couldn't print out the list – only Beth could. You could do screengrabs from the computer screen but the database was controlled by Beth. When Gove jumped ship, how could we crisis-manage 325 Tory MPs with only a few hours left?

We may live in a computer age but the future of the Tory Party, the government and the country ultimately came down to who could print out from whose computer – and a dead-tree letter that Boris failed to deliver to one of his main rivals, Andrea Leadsom.

CHAPTER 11

THE END OF THE AFFAIR: GOVE KNIFES BORIS

The crucial moment – when the whole Johnson–Gove partnership began to collapse – was the afternoon of Wednesday 29 June.

After figuring prominently in the referendum campaign, Andrea Leadsom, until then an unknown energy minister, had emerged as an unlikely big player in the Conservative leadership stakes. That same Wednesday, Johnson and Gove met Leadsom. As a price for supporting Johnson, she demanded to become either Chancellor of the Exchequer or Deputy Prime Minister, leading Brexit negotiations.

Johnson had promised the Chancellor job to Gove, not that he could tell Leadsom that. But, still, both men could in good conscience agree to offer her one of the two other jobs she would accept – Deputy Prime Minister or chief Brexit negotiator. They agreed to the deal over the phone; Leadsom demanded an offer in writing, which Johnson agreed to deliver. He also agreed that he would say, publicly, that evening,

'I am delighted to be joined by Michael Gove and Andrea Leadsom at my launch tomorrow.'

It was on Wednesday, at 5.25 p.m., that Leadsom agreed with Johnson to become one of his top ministers, provided he confirmed it in a tweet and letter by 8 p.m.

When Gove later asked Boris whether he had given the letter to her, Boris discovered he'd left it in his office. It was picked up and delivered to Nick Boles at the Tory Summer Ball at the Hurlingham Club, also attended by Gove and David Cameron. Boles went in search of Leadsom, to discover she had cancelled. Cinderella would not go to the ball – nor would she become the Princess of Downing Street.

By this time, the 8 p.m. deadline for confirmation of the Leadsom deal had been and gone.

At 8.10 p.m., Johnson texted Gove, sitting at another table at the ball, 'Andrea wants me to tweet something like "Looking forward to campaign launch tomorrow with top team Michael Gove and Andrea Leadsom." Is that OK?'

Gove did not reply – which, in the eyes of some Boris allies, proves Gove was already planning his putsch. In any case, Boris had missed Leadsom's deadline.

At 10.15 p.m., Boris left the Hurlingham with Boles. At this crucial moment, Boles had taken Boris's phone – apparently so he could concentrate on writing his speech. In fact, according to Boles's critics, it meant he was in the ideal position to influence the catastrophic events that unfolded over the next three hours.

Once in the car, according to Boles, he read a text on

Boris's phone from Leadsom, sent at 9.38 p.m., saying, 'I am very sorry Boris and Michael but it was very clear that I needed a public statement this evening. I would have been really keen to work with you but I am now going to submit my nomination papers. Best, Andrea.'

An angry Leadsom proceeded to file those papers.

According to Boris, Boles was already filtering the information he was passing back on Boris's mobile, saying to him in the car, 'Andrea has sent a text. There was some cock-up about the tweet.'

An alarmed Boris said, 'Oh fuck, fuck, fuck, what are we going to do?'

Boles texted Gove, saying, 'Something's gone wrong.'

Despite his alarm, Boris says he had no idea that Andrea was actually standing herself at this stage. So he asked Boles to send a text, saying, 'Send her a text to see if we can do it tonight or in the morning.'

The text Boles then sent on Boris's phone to Leadsom certainly made no reference to her standing. It said: 'Sorry, my cockup. I told Boles about the letter, not about the tweet. We can do the tweet now or tomorrow first thing as you prefer.'

By this time, Gove was incensed that Boris had barely started on his leadership speech. By 10 p.m., he had apparently only written 400 words of the 1,500 expected. Boris was still writing it in the car alongside Boles, and continued writing it when he got back to his Islington home. Gove was also angry at the unfolding chaos of the Andrea Leadsom letter/tweet strategy. At the Hurlingham Club, several leading Tories were bending his ear, suggesting he should run against Boris.

Just before 11 p.m., Gove left the Hurlingham and headed to Parliament for discussions with his allies, before making for home in north Kensington. There, just after midnight, he called his closest advisers to a meeting to discuss Boris's behaviour.

'The thing is, Boris isn't that trustworthy,' says a member of Gove's inner circle.

It was clear he wasn't going to stick together with us. He didn't tweet, he didn't bring the letter. Andrea broke ranks first – and that's what triggered Michael to run.

Boris was in nervous breakdown mode. His team were trying to do the speech with him. But he'd left the house with no speech. If you're Prime Minister, you have to do the work. The buck stops with you. You can't be so weak. Michael thought we cannot be this shambolic about everything. Nick Boles thought the same.

Gove and Boris had got along well during the campaign, under the direction of Cummings, but, still, Gove had been exposed for the first time to the Boris school of instinctive, on-the-hoof decision-making.

'During the referendum campaign, Michael had his doubts about Boris's abilities,' says the member of Gove's inner circle.

But they'd Boxed and Coxed quite well. People had suggested

to Michael that he should run, but he was firm that it should just be Boris. Michael thought he could run things behind the scenes, while Boris did the glad-handing and all the public things he's good at.

But Boris couldn't follow through. Everything was falling apart – it was a real shame.

There are many theories about why Gove turned on Boris. Some say it was Lady Macbeth, his wife, goading him on. Some, like Nigel Farage, say he had been planning the coup for weeks; others that Gove had demanded a senior Cabinet position for his old pal George Osborne which wasn't forthcoming. Another theory is that Boris overdid the hospitality on the Vote Leave bus on the way back from a campaign away day – and downloaded to Gove about trouser problems that hadn't yet been picked up by the press. Boris's roving eye – and his love child with Helen Macintyre, an arts consultant – had been well documented. More revelations, if true, might have sunk his leadership bid.

Yet another theory holds that Michael Gove wanted to control all future Cabinet positions, and that when Boris dithered over the letter to Andrea Leadsom, he grasped the nettle – and the long knife. And another suggests Boris's occasional bouts with depression morphed into a meltdown of inactivity, brought on by terror at getting tantalisingly close to the job he'd coveted since childhood.

My own theory is that Gove had been perfectly happy on the campaign trail with Boris when they were both being directed by the very able, authoritative Dominic Cummings. As soon as Boris was the star of the leadership show – and Gove had to rely on him – he realised how unreliable Boris is. He realised that Charles Moore, Margaret Thatcher's biographer, was right about Boris when he borrowed the words used by David Niven of Errol Flynn: 'You knew where you were with Errol Flynn. He always let you down.'

That fits with the view held by senior Tories.

'Boris wasn't ready to be the Prime Minister,' says one of George Osborne's senior advisers.

> He was totally unorganised. They tried to get him to write a speech and he couldn't. He didn't have a proper leadership team around him. He had a couple of junior MPs, and a guy from the BBC. Osborne had an operation. Theresa May had one. Michael was frustrated.
>
> Boris didn't know what he wanted to do as Prime Minister. People were saying to Michael, 'I can't back Boris but I can back you.'

Back to that fatal Wednesday evening. Late that night, Nick Boles received a text from one of Gove's special advisers, asking him to go to Gove's house in north Kensington. Another account suggests he got a call from Gove himself, enraged at Boris's incompetence.

At 12.30 a.m., Boles got an Uber, leaving Boris to grapple with his unfinished speech.

To be forced to write something to a deadline goes right

against Boris's instincts. Particularly when it comes to a speech. I have been at think-tank events where Boris is the star speaker – and, as he enters the room at the last minute, he is still scribbling his speech on a stray piece of A4 while he waits to mount the rostrum.

'Boles and Gove were worried that he hadn't finished his speech yet,' says a close friend of Gove's, 'but they were also worried that what he had written was saying Britain could stay in the Common Market. In other words, he hadn't got Brexit.'

At Gove's home, Boles found three special advisers, Gove and Vine, who had been dining with Simone Finn, a Tory peer and ex-girlfriend of Gove's.

'Michael came back from dinner and said, "I can't in good conscience back Boris,"' said one of Gove's inner circle, who was there that evening. 'We said, "Let's sleep on it."'

Senior figures in UKIP say they were warned about Gove standing at midnight on Wednesday night. The Gove team deny this, saying he only decided to stand on Thursday morning – after Andrea Leadsom put herself forward. Gove was also driven mad by Boris's dithering.

'Michael was just totally fed up with Boris not concentrating, and he realised Boris didn't have any of the qualities to become Prime Minister,' said a member of Gove's inner circle, who was with him on the fatal Wednesday evening he switched sides.

'He saw that Boris was a catastrophe and realised that he was the best of the Brexit candidates who were left,' says another Gove ally, a politician who has known him since Oxford.

At 1.30 a.m., one of the advisers at Gove's house, Henry Cook, rang up Dominic Cummings. Cummings was at home in Islington, preparing to go on holiday the next day with his family.

'Henry says, "I'm here at Michael's house, and Michael's said he's not going to support Boris, he's going to run himself,"' says Cummings. 'I know from that chronology that, at the very least, something happened between the Tuesday breakfast meeting and Wednesday night.'

Cook and two other special advisers had been at Westminster on that Wednesday evening, planning how to make Boris's launch work the next day. At 10 p.m., Cook got a call from Sarah Vine, asking him to come to the Goves' house in north Kensington. When he got there, he was told that Michael wasn't going to back Boris and he was going to run himself.

During that 1.30 a.m. call from the Gove household to Cummings, Nick Boles joined the call on speakerphone.

Cummings says, 'Boles was babbling on about everything blowing up, that Boris was unreliable. He said, "I can't go into it, but a whole lot of things are going to come out about Boris. It's unthinkable, Dominic, that he can be PM."'

Cummings advised Henry Cook that they should all sleep on it.

'I said to Cooky, "Stop drinking, go to bed, get up at seven, regather, ask yourselves if this still looks like a good idea." They were saying they'd decided,' remembers Cummings.

Cummings is convinced Boles was at the heart of Gove's destruction of Boris.

'Boles left Boris's house, saying he was going home, and got in a cab to Michael's house,' says Cummings. 'Everything I've heard makes me absolutely sure that Boles played a critical role somewhere along the line.'

Sarah Vine's role in encouraging Gove to run was crucial. She had been particularly stung when David Cameron had sacked Gove as Education Secretary in July 2014. Cameron denied to me that – as some people say – he sacked Gove as Education Secretary because his election guru, Lynton Crosby, was disappointed by Gove's polling.

'You need to move people around from time to time and I wanted a very strong Chief Whip,' Cameron said. 'It was the right time. I moved Michael because the agenda I backed 100 per cent – and is still being put in place. Free schools, independent schools within the state sector, curriculum reform, examination reform, discipline reform.'

It was critical, too, that, all that Wednesday afternoon and evening, Nick Boles was in charge of Boris's mobile.

'Boris said it was complete bollocks, bullshit from Boles, that he hadn't finished his piece,' says Cummings.

Boris said, 'Boles had my phone all afternoon and night. The text message came in and Boles told me what Leadsom's text message said. And I told him what to reply. He left at 12.30 a.m. He told me he was going home. In fact, he left to go to Gove's house. I looked at the phone. What the fuck's going on? What you told me is not Leadsom's text, what I told you to reply is not the reply you gave.'

Boris said Boles invented the text from Leadsom, and invented the reply, and then gave the whole bullshit story to the media. Michael is stunned by this story. Boles pulled a fast one. Both got suckered by a scumbag and didn't know what they were dealing with.

I was astonished Boles was in the room, never mind the campaign manager. Every person said to me, 'Boles was disastrous. Useless, incompetent.' Ten or twelve Vote Leave people said absolutely the same thing.

Why would you have Boles running round with your mobile phone? It definitely shouldn't be Nick Boles in charge of the next Prime Minister's phone.

Cummings continues:

I've got a hunch Boles went there at 12.30 a.m. and gave a strongly exaggerated story, makes things up, to say, 'Look at this useless man, you can't have a guy like this in charge of nuclear weapons. You've got to do this tomorrow. This guy is totally fucked. The whole thing's going to blow up sky high. This is what he's done wrong with Leadsom.'

Michael would trust Boles completely. It would not occur to Michael that Boles would invent shit.

A friend of Gove's says:

Michael persuaded himself Boris would be a disaster. Boles

had wound him up. A lot of people said to Michael, 'You're the intellectual godfather of Vote Leave. You made the arguments. Boris was the showman. You were the brains of the operation.' Boles said on Wednesday to Michael, 'All these people will come over to you.'

Other insiders claim Gove made the decision to knife Boris out of altruism.

'Gove decided to fall on his sword in an anything-but-Boris move,' says a close friend of Nick Boles.

In the end, out of all the reasons proposed for Gove's attack on Boris, it is this – Boris's unsuitability for high office – that led to the knifing.

'Michael's public and private story are essentially that the way Boris operated between Tuesday morning, and the next two days, [led to the conclusion that] "I looked at this guy and thought he cannot be in Downing Street,"' says Dominic Cummings. 'The night before, he clearly got into his head a picture of, "I must do this to save the country from Boris."'

Certainly, there was a change in the efficiency of the operation once the referendum campaign was over, and Boris was ostensibly in charge.

'We'd all dealt with Boris for several months – he's got lots of qualities; some he's not so good at,' says Cummings. 'Man management in the fashion of Bill Gates has never been his strong point. That's why we did the deal that we'd be in charge of civil service reform. That's not a reason to pull the plug on him.'

There is another factor – the fact that Andrea Leadsom was now being taken seriously as a leadership candidate, after the affair of the missing letter. For someone like Michael Gove – of Olympian intelligence, who had been in the inner circles of power for six years – to defer to Andrea Leadsom – not of Olympian intelligence, never in those inner circles of power – offended his *amour-propre*.

'At the end of the day, Michael's a straight, honest guy,' says Victoria Woodcock, Vote Leave's director of operations, who went on to work on Gove's leadership campaign. 'And I believe him when he said he could no longer support Boris. Knowing how loyal he is, that must have been the hardest decision to make.'

In the end, it was a combination of all these factors that led Gove to unsheathe his dagger: the chaos of Boris's leadership campaign; the encouragement of Sarah Vine and Nick Boles; the knowledge of his own talent and experience; and the knowledge of Leadsom's lack of both.

And now to the fatal Thursday 30 June – the day of Boris's downfall.

At 7 a.m. that day, Gove's campaign manager asked MPs to come to Gove's leadership launch. Still, at 7.08 a.m., a Gove adviser emailed Johnson's team, assuring them Gove's supporters would be at Boris's launch.

'Michael made no final decision on standing until the next morning, when he called Boris,' says a member of Gove's inner circle, who was there that fateful evening. 'He couldn't get through, so he called Lynton Crosby next.'

Johnson's team claim he never received the call but only heard the news from Lynton Crosby. Gove called Crosby at 8.45 a.m. on Thursday.

'Lynton, I'm running,' Gove said.

'Running what?' said Crosby.

'I'm running for the leadership myself.'

'Crosby told us in short, Australian terms: "He's done us over,"' a senior member of Boris's campaign team said.

At 8.54 a.m. we got an email from Nick Boles saying he couldn't fill in the nomination papers, and he emailed the blank forms.

Boles clearly never intended to get them completed. Gove knew this when, on Wednesday morning, he insisted Boles take charge of the nomination process.

I've got no objection to Gove jumping ship. It was the manner in which he did it. It was designed to cause maximum problems. At every single step, they stitched Boris up. Gove wanted to maximise his chances and minimise Boris's. Of course, Gove always wanted to be PM. Gove only believes in Gove.

After talking to Gove, Crosby rang Johnson to tell him the news.

'Well, that's it,' Boris said. 'I can't go on. I can't run.'

Crosby encouraged Boris to hold fire and come into the Westminster office.

At 9.02 a.m., Gove released a statement, saying, 'I have come reluctantly to the conclusion that Boris cannot provide the leadership or build the team for the task ahead. I have, therefore, decided to put my name forward for the leadership.'

Soon after, Boris took soundings from Crosby, who apparently said, 'Get out fast,' once he'd run the numbers on Boris's leadership chances. The previous night, Boris had had ninety-seven MPs' votes; by that morning, it had slumped to thirty-eight.

Crosby knows whereof he speaks: he turned down offers to run the losing Zac Goldsmith mayoral run and the Remain campaign. There are rumours, too, that he turned down a £2 million offer to run the Leave campaign – not because he thought they would lose, but because he was advising so many Remain donors that it would have been impolitic to do so.

Dominic Cumming says:

The main story [explaining why Boris stood down] is Lynton said, 'If you stand, you're fucked. But, if you resign, no one's ever going to know if you could have won, and the mystique is still there. And you live to fight another day.'

Lynton probably did tell him that. He really listens to Lynton much more than I realised.

Somebody who has worked with Boris in journalism says, 'Boris kind of believes in ghosts, the Greek gods, pigeon entrails. Lynton is his soothsayer.'

Boris adjourned to a room with his wife, Marina, where he decided to stand down.

'He then gave a great speech and showed the bastards what they were missing,' says a senior member of Boris's campaign team.

At 11.40 a.m., Boris arrived at St Ermin's Hotel in Westminster. Instead of making his launch speech, he said to the unknowing MPs, eleven minutes in, 'Having consulted colleagues, and in view of the circumstances in Parliament, I have concluded that person [the next Tory leader] cannot be me.'

Soon after, David Cameron sent Johnson a text: 'You should have stuck with me, mate.'

Boris spent the following weekend visiting Cornwall, fulfilling long-standing commitments to visit Tory constituency associations – commitments that were made before his leadership bid.

'Some of the constituencies have MPs that support Theresa May but he honoured his commitments,' said a source close to Boris, who is confident that he will fight for the leadership again one day.

The following Monday, Boris's *Telegraph* column was crammed with tips on how to run the country. He remains popular with Tory members and is still thirteen years younger than Churchill when he became PM. The second act in Boris's career began with his appointment by May as Foreign Secretary.

'He's landed on his feet,' says Nigel Farage. 'He's got one of the great offices of state. I wish him well.'

But why did Boris stand down so quickly? Nigel Farage has two possible suggestions.

'With Leadsom still in the game, because he'd been busy playing cricket, and not phoned her, the numbers weren't there – that's one interpretation,' says Farage. 'The other interpretation [is] that there were a lot more stories about to come out. That there were two more kids. One illegitimate child is OK. Another two. That's stretching it a bit.'

Another theory is that Theresa May dangled the plum job of Foreign Secretary as a consolation prize for standing down. Insiders, though, say that is unlikely. Right up until the moment Boris was offered the Foreign Secretary job, he thought his political career was over and that he wasn't in favour with Theresa May.

The other factor is Boris's character. For all his deep-seated confidence, his ambition to be world king, there are chinks in the armour. Like his idol, Winston Churchill, he is prey to the black dog of depression. In the depths of one of his momentary glooms, exacerbated by Gove's knifing, his confidence could well have flickered and dimmed.

Boris also has a longing to be liked – thus the stream of jokes. Gove's dagger blow is hardly a sign of affection; and the thought that MPs wouldn't gather round him for the leadership contest would have shaken his confidence even more. Abusive crowds had been gathering outside Johnson's Islington house since the referendum. That shook him – and his wife and children.

Still, senior Tories were astonished that Boris decided to pull out.

'It was a very odd decision,' says a senior adviser of George Osborne's.

For the rest of his life, he'll wonder what would have happened if he'd stood.

Even if he'd been told he wouldn't win, there was so much uncertainty. Think about all the extraordinary things that had happened in the previous week. Osborne hadn't run; Michael had backed Boris and then refused to back him. There would have been another two months of a contest. OK, he might not have won, but he had a chance.

He didn't even have to say what he was going to do with the job. He just has to say he's Boris Johnson.

One thing's for sure – the dagger thrust went deep, even if the two men are now on speaking terms once more.

'Boris is now talking to Gove,' a close friend of Boris's told me in early September 2016.

'Johnsons don't hate,' said another close friend of the Johnson clan, 'but Boris can never, ever forgive him for what he did.'

Other wounds have also healed. George Osborne has made up with Michael Gove and Steve Hilton, Cameron's former senior adviser, who came out for Leave.

'It was very difficult,' says a senior adviser of Osborne's. 'It was more of an internecine civil war than a general election, when you're less likely to have friends on the other side. It wasn't pleasant. George has largely patched it up. It will take longer for David Cameron to patch things up with Gove.'

Why did Michael Gove wield the knife – and wield it so late? Nigel Farage is in no doubt about the timing of the dagger thrust.

'That's when you do it, isn't it, to be most effective?' he says.

The confusing thing is that the assassination goes against Michael Gove's character. I can't claim to know him at all well – but I have bumped into him, on and off, for around seventeen years. He has always been unfailingly polite – if anything, polite to a fault, so perfect are his manners, so beautifully turned his words. I have seen him give prepared wedding speeches – and a completely impromptu speech at a 30th birthday party, which was just as precise and funny as the prepared speech.

'I think Michael is one of the most decent people in politics,' says Douglas Carswell.

I know where he's been. You've got to be prepared to break friendships to do what you think's right. I did that when I left the Tory Party. You shouldn't choose what you do on the basis of who's going to invite you to dinner.

I think that's what Michael did. Michael said he wouldn't stand but he came to realise that he's as entitled to have a crack at being Prime Minister as anyone.

Michael Gove finds it very hard to say no. When I tried to interview him for this book, he said several times in emails that he would meet me, despite embarking on his own book about the whole thing himself. When I bumped into him in that Covent Garden restaurant in September 2016, he was politeness itself, still agreeing to be interviewed – but he could never agree to a time. Rather than say no, he did the much more polite thing – of constantly saying yes, without being pinned down.

I told this to a BBC film-maker and he said:

> That's nothing! Michael's been agreeing to do interviews with me for six years, and never has. The last time I told him about an interview request he'd agreed to, he said, 'Oh, I'm sorry, it must have got lost in the dreadful silt of government.' He's so polite, and his apologies are so good, that you always forgive him.

Nick Boles was pivotal in the whole operation. It is striking that he arrived at Boris's house on the Wednesday night on his side – and left for Michael Gove's house that same evening, having switched sides.

It fits with my only dealings with Boles. Fifteen years ago, when I was working on the *Daily Telegraph* comment desk, one of my jobs was to line up a series of opinion pieces between Christmas and New Year – when there was only a skeleton staff in the office.

Boles, then a Westminster councillor, had agreed long before that he would file a piece for that dead period between Christmas and New Year.

I rang him to check he was filing the piece.

'So sorry,' he said, 'I haven't been able to do it.'

It was annoying – but, still, after a bit of ringing round, I found a substitute.

The next day I was astonished to see exactly the piece that had been commissioned, appearing in *The Times*. It was one thing to write a piece for a rival paper – quite another to lie through his teeth that he wasn't going to write one at all.

I shouldn't have been so surprised, then, at the Boles switcheroo from Johnson to Gove. It was in his character. And character dictated everything in the whole saga of the referendum and the Tory leadership campaign.

In the classical terms Boris loves, the Brexit curse was like the Greek tragedy word '*hamartia*' – the fatal character flaw that leads to hubris that leads to nemesis. All the main players were under such pressure that they were struck down by their core weaknesses. Cameron and Osborne – so buoyed by their general election and Scottish referendum victories – were lulled into complacency, thinking negative tactics would work once more. Boris was brought down by his lack of organisation. And Gove was felled by a momentary over-estimation of his capacity for absolute power.

As Boris will also know, it is hubris that, in Greek tragedy, inexorably leads to nemesis. The last act of the tragedy was about to unfold.

CHAPTER 12

NO, PRIME MINISTER: GOVE IMPLODES

It wasn't just that Gove assassinated Boris; it's the way he did it.

What stuck in many MPs' throats was the manner of that statement he gave on Thursday 30 June 2016 – 'Boris cannot provide the leadership or build the team for the task ahead.'

Dominic Cummings says:

If Michael had said from the beginning, 'Boris is a hero, the main reason we won, a friend of mine, but we've got different views about how the country should be run, I'm going to run for leader as well as him, we'll do it in the best of spirits, we have a different view, the public can make their mind up,' a whole bunch of MPs might have said, 'We want Michael Gove.' The crucial psychological fuck-up Boles and co. made was thinking they could stab Boris in the back, and then all the people would go and back Michael.

What they actually did was go, 'What the fuck have you

guys just done? There's got to be something wrong with you lot. There's something very distasteful about it. I'm going to vote for someone else.'

As a result of taking Boris out, Gove's subsequent leadership campaign never got off the ground – over the course of its brief life, it always had the scent of death around it.

A Gove leadership office was set up by Nick Boles on Thursday 30 June. There was a desperate scramble for office space, suggesting that the assassination had indeed been last-minute.

'We worked out of some guy's flat in Westminster,' says Cleo Watson, who went to work on Gove's leadership campaign. 'It definitely didn't feel planned at all. I kept laughing at that idea. If anyone could come into this office for five minutes, they would see what an absolute joke it was.'

The new office was so quickly cobbled together – with only six people working there, and a tiny budget – that no one was given an official job title. Gove advisers got together to work on the message of the campaign and to sketch out speeches.

'I'm not sure I ever thought we would get through but, if we did, I thought there was a chance we could take on May,' says Victoria Woodcock, who had been an adviser to Gove when he was Chief Whip, and came to work on his leadership bid.

Knowing how things were going with Andrea Leadsom, and with the back-stabbing thing, it seemed unlikely. If we'd had Dom [Cummings], maybe we could have brought it back.

I was so frustrated. I couldn't even get people to agree on a slogan. I had twenty ideas. Who was making the decisions round here? Ultimately, it was Nick Boles. Which wasn't the right answer. He's not a campaign director.

On 4 July, Johnson endorsed Leadsom for leader. Gove made it through the first leadership round on 5 July, when Liam Fox was eliminated.

'What was incredibly clear was those MPs weren't going to forgive him,' says Cleo Watson.

If he'd even had another weekend to talk MPs around, maybe that would have helped. It's a numbers game. There's no point in trying to find office space, if you know you're not going to get your MPs.

We didn't think he'd win and we didn't think it was a good thing he'd done but we really like Michael, basically. I don't think any of us thought he'd win.

The Gove team, made up of old friends and colleagues, worked on his bid out of loyalty and affection. But it was always doomed – because he had become known as the Brutus of the leadership race, and because his entry was so late.

'It could have been different if Gove had decided to stand from the beginning,' says Victoria Woodcock. 'Because he made such a late decision, I knew it was going to be an uphill battle.'

Nick Boles tried to bring over May supporters to Gove

with a text before the final run-off leadership vote on 7 July
2016. Boles's text read:

> I respect the fact that you want Theresa May to be the Prime
> Minister. It is overwhelmingly likely that she will be, and if
> she does I will sleep easily at night. But I am seriously fright-
> ened about the risk of allowing Andrea Leadsom onto the
> membership ballot.
>
> What if Theresa stumbles? Are we really confident that
> the membership won't vote for a fresh face who shares their
> attitudes about much of modern life, like they did with IDS?
>
> Michael doesn't mind spending two months taking a good
> thrashing from Theresa if that is what it takes but in the par-
> ty's interest and the national interest, surely we must all work
> together to stop AL?

Boles's tactical text didn't work. In the second round on 7 July,
Gove was eliminated with forty-six votes, leaving Andrea
Leadsom (eighty-four votes) and Theresa May (199 votes) as
the final pair in the race. Before they could be voted on by
party members, Leadsom stood down on 11 July, leaving May
as the only candidate.

Despite being a Remainer, May's first few months as Prime
Minister have been surprisingly popular among some of the
dedicated Brexiteers.

'I don't think Theresa May's put a foot wrong,' says Douglas Carswell.

I've got quite a soft spot for her. I think she's wonderful. It's maths. We've only got a slender majority in the Commons for Brexit. Think of all those strident Remainers. Who's more likely to get them through the division lobbies? Andrea Leadsom or Theresa May?

From the moment the Tories had their leadership contest, I thought that a grown-up Remainer who won't fall flat on their face and who will do a good job of governance, and who will get Brexit through, if that means a lot of ghastly Remainers getting junior ministerial jobs, if that's what it takes, then so be it.

I asked Nigel Farage whether he was happy with the three Brexiteers – Boris Johnson, Liam Fox and David Davis – who have been entrusted with seeing Brexit through.

'Oh God, yeah – very much so,' he says.

And is he happy with Theresa May?

'Course not,' he said,

but everything she's said so far is good. Mind you, everything she said as Home Secretary on immigration was good, and she didn't follow through. We shall see.

As I said to the two lads from Sunderland yesterday who bought me a beer, 'If, by the time of the next general election, you in Sunderland have got your 200-mile exclusive zone, like the Norwegians, and that fish market [in Sunderland] is full of thousands of boxes of fish every morning, we'll know we've won.'

CHAPTER 13

TWILIGHT OF THE NOTTING HILL SET: CAMERON'S CAMELOT CRUMBLES

'Don't let it be forgot that once there was a spot, for one brief, shining moment, that was known as Camelot.'

So wrote Alan Jay Lerner in the 1960 musical about King Arthur's magical castle and court. Jackie Kennedy so loved the production that she referred to John F. Kennedy's three brief years in the White House as Camelot.

23 June 2016 marked a sudden end to David Cameron's Camelot. Like JFK, Cameron was a youthful forty-three when he came to office. Like JFK, he has a stylish wife and charming young children. And, like JFK, he had his time in office cut short, if not quite so brutally.

It was quite a fall from grace for the most successful Tory leader since Margaret Thatcher.

According to one old Oxford friend of his, 'David Cameron

was the man who made all middle-aged public schoolboys jealous.'

Another contemporary from Eton said of his time at school, 'He was arrogant in a sea of arrogance.'

Speaking as a middle-aged public schoolboy myself, I'm neither jealous of him nor do I think he's arrogant – but that's because I'm his second cousin, and have benefited from his success.

Cameron let me interview him four times during his tenure as Conservative leader. I followed him from the SAS HQ outside Hereford, to the First World War battlefields of the Western Front, to the ASDA in the shadow of the Wolves ground in Wolverhampton. I interviewed him so often, in fact, that an editor at the *Daily Mail* once called me the Terry Major-Ball of Cameron's premiership.

In 2010, Cameron was mocked for referring to himself and his wife as belonging to the 'sharp-elbowed middle classes'. I could see exactly what he meant. Yes, to the outside world, Cameron, a baronet's grandson, and his wife, a baronet's daughter, look upper-class. Speaking as a baronet's son, you do feel middle-class if – as the Camerons and I do – you bump into the real upper classes and see quite how much richer and grander they are. By comparison, you feel tremendously middle class. I know it sounds ridiculous – but the whole ludicrous class system depends to a great extent on where you feel you stand in the dreary old rankings.

Cameron, though, undeniably came from what you might call the influence classes: the mixture of politicians, journalists, publishers and businessmen that came to be known as the Notting Hill Set.

Their high point began in their late thirties and early forties in 2005, when Cameron became Tory leader. It's not as if they were flung into the gutter on 24 June 2016, when Cameron resigned. But their moment in the glare of the sun had passed. Until referendum day, they were a charmed, glittering clique, blessed with the accidental gift of perfect timing.

In 2010, after thirteen years of Labour, the country was ready for a Tory government – and Cameron, at forty-three, and George Osborne, at thirty-eight, were just the right age, after years of toiling in the salt mines of Conservative Central Office and Parliament.

It's hard to think of a Prime Minister and Chancellor who have got on so well, in office and afterwards. On 14 July 2016, the day after Cameron left Downing Street, he was having coffee with Osborne in – where else? – the northern fringes of Notting Hill.

The beating heart of Tory thought, from the mid-1990s until 23 June, was this gilded corner of west London – stretching from the Holland Park house of Sir Alan Parker, the Brunswick PR tycoon who lent his home to the Camerons after they left Downing Street, to the Osbornes' Notting Hill house and to the north Kensington houses of the Camerons and the Goves.

It's striking how Boris Johnson, the one Bullingdon big beast to survive, and be promoted in Theresa May's first reshuffle, was never part of the set. That's not just because he lives in Islington, north London. He is also two years older than Cameron and – despite that famous Bullingdon photograph – never knew him well at Eton or Oxford.

Johnson, for all his jolly affability, is a loner at heart, happier giving speeches than going to dinner parties. At one such gathering, tired with the conversation, he said to the women on either side of him: 'Look, this isn't going too well. Shall I just give a speech instead?'

He is strangely unclubbable, even if he did join the Bullingdon. That might be what saved him when the Notting Hill Set were binned after the referendum. Because he was never a member of the club of insiders, he wasn't a member of the *salon des refusés* either.

The Notting Hill Set, on the other hand, were an intensely sociable group who studied, holidayed and worked together. Their friendships were close, often going back to their undergraduate days at Oxford.

Funnily enough, before they moved into politics, the set didn't talk about politics much on the occasions I bumped into them. I was in the same year as Osborne at Magdalen College, Oxford – where we both studied history – and he never once mentioned a desire to go into politics.

Neither Osborne nor Cameron bothered much with the Oxford Union, the traditional cradle of aspiring politicians. That explains Cameron's sunny normality, on show in his last Prime Minister's Questions on 13 July 2016. He was never the eccentric fourteen-year-old devouring Hansard under the bedclothes. Politics was never everything to him. Saddened though he was by his fall, he won't go into Incredible Sulk mode, à la Gordon Brown or Edward Heath.

As his family farewell to Downing Street showed, Cameron is devoted to his wife and children. He really will be content to pick up a few directorships and settle back, once the tenants have left, into his Notting Hill home.

'He'll return to his life with Sam, and things won't change much,' says one old friend. 'Other politicians' personal lives are far more dependent on their careers.'

He would have been perfectly happy to stay on as a backbencher but realised it was impossible.

'He was genuinely planning to stay on,' one of his senior aides told me, 'but, once he stood down, he knew it would become impossible. Any time he disagreed with government policy, it would just make things difficult.'

There are indications, too, that Theresa May wanted Cameron to clear off pretty sharpish.

'He asked if he could give a farewell to supporters at the Tory conference in October, but he was told in no uncertain terms by May's people that he couldn't,' says a friend of Cameron's.

The Notting Hill Set's friendships often predated their political ambitions and they are all the stronger for that. But, as the set moved into politics, those friendships – and their Notting Hill houses – became the springboard into the big time. Over one another's dinner tables they plotted the Tory revival after the long exile of the Blair years.

It's easy to forget what an outsider Cameron was when

he sparked that revival – by standing against David Davis for the party leadership in 2005. It wasn't even certain that he would be the one to grasp the nettle. Cameron discussed with Osborne whether the latter should run instead.

Cameron told me in an interview for the *Sunday Times* in April 2015:

> George and I talked about it because we're close friends. He said, 'You should go for it.' He'd thought about it and decided not to. There was no Granita-style pact. He'd been made shadow Chancellor, he was very keen on that. We had a very amicable, open conversation about it. Because I was thinking, should I, shouldn't I, and he thought I should, and he wasn't going to. We'd kind of agreed we'd work together.

And they did – for the next eleven years. Cameron's loyalty to his old friends and his staff is unusual. He had the same principal advisers on his last day in office as he did on his first day as Conservative leader in 2005: Ed Llewellyn, his chief of staff, and Kate Fall, his deputy chief of staff, both at Oxford with him; Liz Sugg, his head of operations; and Gabby Bertin, his head of external relations and former press aide.

All were made peers in Cameron's controversial resignation honours list (apart from Kate Fall, who was ennobled in 2015). It is rumoured some of them may join a putative Cameron foundation continuing his work on the 'Big Society'.

That loyalty had its down side. Cameron should have got rid of Andy Coulson – the former *News of the World* editor, jailed for phone hacking – as his communications director long before he did. That resignation honours – with peerages and knighthoods for his inner circle – only buttressed the idea of a chumocracy at the heart of power. You can see why backbench MPs, locked out of the magic circle of Cameron's friends, weren't so enamoured of him.

You can see, too, why there was a mass defenestration of the Notting Hill Set after the referendum. They had risen together as they gathered power; when power vanished, all the princes of Camelot were bound to fall as one.

But why did Cameron call the referendum – and so bring the spires and turrets of Camelot crashing down to the ground?

CHAPTER 14

THE CAMERON YEARS: WHEN THE LUCK RAN OUT

It's only with the benefit of hindsight that David Cameron's decision to hold a referendum looks catastrophic. In fact, at the time, it made a sort of sense.

To lose the referendum, Cameron had to be both very lucky and very unlucky: that is, win a highly unlikely majority at the 2015 election, which would trigger the referendum; and then lose the referendum – also an unlikely prospect.

Until 2016, Cameron had had the best of luck: coming of political age at just the right time, after thirteen years when the Tories were in the wilderness; lucky in his opponents, Gordon Brown and Ed Miliband; lucky in the electoral collapse of Labour, particularly in Scotland; lucky, too, in the result of the Scottish referendum, which looked, at one point, in danger of going against him.

Project Fear, driven largely by George Osborne as Chancellor, also made a certain sense. The negative campaigning

for the Scottish referendum and the 2015 election worked –
why shouldn't it work again?

'George did what he did because he had a lot to lose, as
subsequent events showed,' says Douglas Carswell. 'Tactics.'

A close friend of George Osborne's says he thinks the referendum shows that the whole matrix of politics he cut his
teeth on has changed.

'George thinks political parties have religiously followed the
1992 Clinton idea – that you poll, stick to one message and
drum it home,' says Osborne's friend. 'That worked for Blair
with Philip Gould [New Labour's polling and strategy guru
in five general elections, from 1987 to 2005]. But social media
and a general aggression to politicians has changed all that.'

In other words, a disconnect has grown up between the
people and the politicians – a well-documented phenomenon that accounts for Brexit and the Trump victory, along
with the far-right and far-left fringe groups that have sprung
to prominence across Europe.

But why didn't Cameron spot all this? Is there some fundamental flaw in his character? Some fatal streak of hubris?

'David Cameron is one of the cleverest people I've ever
met, and very charming,' says Douglas Carswell.

He's got one small flaw – he's got a naturally competitive
streak to him. And he can't take being corrected. If you can't
take being corrected, it's fine if you're in the officer corps, because there'll be plenty of brother officers who'll tell you why
you're talking baloney. But if you become the Field Marshal,

and you can't be corrected, your blunders can become catastrophic if you're not good at taking advice.

Carswell, who used to work in Brussels, once suggested to
Cameron that he should get rid of 'UKRep' – the United
Kingdom Permanent Representation to the European Union,
which represents the UK in negotiations with the EU.

'They're dreadful,' says Carswell. 'I said to David Cameron, "Put someone you trust in as the new head, and get them
to have a confirmation hearing in front of MPs to reassure
your party." He was totally dismissive of it.'

Carswell also suggested to Cameron some changes and reforms to the EU before his Bloomberg speech in January 2013.

'I was completely brushed aside and dismissed,' says Carswell.
'He needn't have listened to me, as a pipsqueak. If he'd listened
to more grown-up people, he'd probably still be Prime Minister.'

I can't say Cameron has ever been dismissive of me – but,
again, that may just be politeness to a cousin. In my five years
as the deputy comment editor of the *Daily Telegraph*, he was
the only politician ever to write a thank-you letter to me, for
commissioning an article from him.

'He's extremely good at flattery,' says Andrew Gimson,
Boris Johnson's biographer.

He made a point of coming up to me to say how much he'd
laughed at one of my articles. He's got extraordinarily good
manners. At an event with the Chelsea Pensioners with Boris,
one of the pensioners fell over and got stuck behind a fence.

No one noticed, but Cameron immediately rushed over, even though he was in the middle of talking to the Lieutenant Governor. 'Sir, can I help you?' Cameron said to the pensioner.

Cameron has old-fashioned manners, particularly when it comes to older people. I saw them in action when I followed him on a 2006 visit to Plas Bellin, a centre for homeless families in Flintshire, north Wales. The centre was chaired by Edna Speed, a tough woman in her seventies who set up the charity forty years ago.

As we left, after Cameron had given a speech launching the Tories' Welsh manifesto, he rushed back to Mrs Speed and said, 'Thank you very much for having me' – a particular form of words inculcated in the typical English gentleman schoolboy. The well-brought-up boy might say it after tea with a great-aunt or a weekend's stay in a grand country house.

Other journalists talk about how his manners can be selective; how he can be abrupt to unimportant people; how he doesn't say thank you to minor operatives.

'He's not like the other Tory MPs,' one political journalist told me. 'He never gets drunk. He had me round to dinner and was friendly but patronising. He's really an old-fashioned patrician. That's what Old Etonians are like these days: they used to be shambolic, and now they're very competitive, under a thin veneer of self-deprecation.'

'He defers to no one professionally, except perhaps Kate Fall because she's the gatekeeper,' says one close friend. 'And he defers to Sam; she's got an inner steel.'

Cameron's staff, however, wouldn't hear a word against him when I cross-questioned them.

'He inspires leader-worship in lots of us,' one senior Tory adviser told me.

Cameron is also unusually jolly for a politician – thus that famous humming incident as he entered Downing Street on 11 July, when he had just confirmed he would stand down and hand over to Theresa May.

With the press on the battle bus during the 2010 election debates, he kept up a steady supply of banter throughout the day, occasionally dropping into the chorus of Take That's 'I Want You Back', after our meeting that morning with Take That's Gary Barlow, a Tory supporter.

'Sam gave me a congratulatory kiss after the debate,' he told us, leaning on the headrests either side of the aisle, as we trundled through north Wales. 'But the rest of the evening will remain confidential, part of the marital contract.'

While he teases in conversation, in his speeches he goes in for self-deprecating humour. He introduced Gary Barlow in Nantwich that morning by saying, 'Last night, on the telly debate, I sometimes felt I was part of Britain's worst boyband. That's why I am so pleased to share a stage with a member of Britain's best-ever boyband.'

The banter only broke down into a flash of tetchy anger once that day, when a lobby journalist asked him about the narrowing polls.

'My job is to move the dial, not to set the pointer,' Cameron said, not quite snapping, but almost.

That calm manner of Cameron's – and his unlined, rosy complexion – led to rumours of his chillaxing, of government by essay crisis. In fact, that was unfair – he was always up at dawn, powering through the red boxes.

He is efficient with his time. I remember staying at a house in Northumberland with him in 2003, when he was a backbench MP. We had all just got in from a freezing Saturday's shooting, and were heading off for a bath or a cup of tea. Cameron snatched up his phone and there, on the spot, in front of all the lazybones types, including me, settling into armchairs, he did a live radio interview. It was about a disability bill he was trying to get through Parliament.

His son, Ivan, had been born the previous year, with Ohtahara syndrome, which means he regularly had a series of debilitating fits which could last for as long as an hour. The seizures gradually become more frequent and bring with them major physical retardation and cerebral palsy. Ivan couldn't crawl, walk or talk. He died in 2009, aged six.

Cameron showed the same hyper-pragmatic approach to time management when I followed him on a plane to the Western Front for the centenary of the beginning of the First World War. We were visiting the memorial to a great-great-uncle of David Cameron's – and mine: Captain Francis Mount, killed on the last day of the Battle of Loos in October 1915.

Cameron's advisers, his protection officer and Sajid Javid, then Culture Secretary, were all squeezed together on a tiny private jet. We were flying from Glasgow – where a morning centenary service had been held in Glasgow Cathedral – to Charleroi Airport in Belgium.

After Cameron had read through the brief for the day's events, he said, 'Right,' collapsed his seat, which unfolded into a flatbed, and fell instantly into a deep sleep, inches away from my face.

In another interview, I asked him whether he worried at night and had difficulty sleeping.

'Oh no – I fall asleep before my head hits the pillow,' he said.

That confidence and lack of anxiety have always been his most striking characteristics.

Cameron is five years older than me, but he didn't take advantage of his superiority in age to belittle me at family gatherings. He was untouched, too, by adolescent bolshiness. He was no goody-goody, though: he took the edge off his unfailing politeness with little blasts of conspiratorial gossip, as he still does.

For as long as I can remember, he has appeared untouched by self-doubt or gloom; an irrepressibly chatty soul, with in-exhaustible supplies of energy and enthusiasm.

My enduring memory of my first interview with him in 2006, a year after he became leader of the Tories, was on a helicopter flight from Battersea to north Wales to visit an aircraft factory.

As our helicopter moved in to land at Hawarden, the rotor blades whirred so loudly that no one could hear each other speak. Cameron was sitting next to Cheryl Gillan, then shadow Secretary of State for Wales. Cameron turned to her and, without a word, gently took her wrist.

Still silent, Cameron, who wasn't wearing a watch, flipped Gillan's wrist and looked at her watch, which she wore on her palm side. Again, without a word, he turned her wrist back round and prepared for landing.

Gillan looked a little shocked at first but, once she worked out what he wanted, she grinned, pleased to have been of service. The gesture spoke volumes about Cameron's character: ruthlessly efficient with time, self-aware, aware of the character of others, sure of what he wants and unafraid to do what is necessary to get it.

'Lots of people go into politics because they weren't popular at school, or were bullied,' says Daniel Hannan, the Conservative MEP. 'That's not the case with him. He's doing it because he honestly thinks he can do it better than the current lot.'

That confidence is buttressed by his imposing physical presence. He is taller in the flesh and chunkier than you'd expect, usually dressed in a dark blue suit with a white shirt. He is a bit plump, but not fat, with two small chins shadowing the main one. Despite smoking regularly for twenty years (he's now given up), he has rosy, unlined skin that doesn't need much shaving; crow's-feet appear around his eyes when he smiles. Towards the end of his term in office, though, he began to look a little exhausted, with dark lines under his eyes.

In summer, there's a touch of farmer's neck – a tan line parallel with his shirt collar. His eyes are dark blue, with a touch of melancholy. When he's concentrating, he pulls in his thin upper lip. His hair is flecked with grey, particularly over the ears. He has a small bald patch, about the size of a 50p piece, concealed by swept-back hair.

As he gives speeches, he splays his fingers, holding his broad hands out in front of him like he's carrying a bag of peat. When he wants to make a point, he pushes out the top knuckle of his right index finger with his thumb, thrusting it towards the audience. As he hammers out the point, he breaks up his sentences with mini karate blows on the lectern: 'These are the. Last. Ditch. Lies. Of a government that is. Running out of. Ideas.'

As I spent two days on the election trail with him in the spring of 2015, that confidence remained unruffled. The only time he looked a bit out of sorts was when the buffet trolley clattered down the aisle of the 8.43 a.m. from Euston to Birmingham New Street.

'God, those bacon sandwiches smell good,' he said, turning them down because he was on 'just a little bit' of a diet. He'd lost two kilos – he chose metric over imperial – since Christmas, through sporadic jogging and dieting: on our other day trip, he had a supermarket salad for lunch.

Our conversation rolled along at an easygoing, jokey, anecdotal pace. When I passed on some gossip, he said, 'Oh, is she?' with roguish, Terry-Thomas emphasis.

He burst out laughing when I tell him we're thirteenth cousins of Kim Kardashian. A few weeks later, he dropped the fact into an interview with *Heat* magazine.

Asked whether he watched *Keeping Up with the Kardashians*, Cameron said, 'No, but I'm related to them. Did you know I'm thirteenth cousins with them?'

The strangest thing about David Cameron is that he isn't strange. For all the privilege, it's hard to locate the childhood slight, the teenage will to power, the leader complex that propelled him into Parliament and on to Downing Street.

Admittedly, Cameron's mother's family were active in Conservative politics for 140 years. Cameron's great-grandfather, great-great-grandfather and great-great-great-grandfather were all Tory MPs, going back to 1818. Still, none of them could claim nearly as much political success as the younger William's great-grandson, David Cameron. The highest office any of them attained was as Parliamentary Private Secretary to two Chancellors of the Exchequer at the turn of the nineteenth century.

There were echoes of his ancestors' politics scattered around the family home in Berkshire. Hanging on the wall of the kitchen was a leaflet by the Liberal opponent of Cameron's great-grandfather – William Mount, Tory MP for Newbury – in the 1906 election.

'It was a very good negative attack leaflet,' says Cameron.

'Mr Mount's votes for expensive food.' It listed all the votes he'd cast for protection: '1d on sugar, 2d on bread. Vote Mackarness [the Liberal opponent] for free trade, retrenchment and reform.' It was an early Lib Dem attack. And it was a landslide. He lost in 1906. Got back in 1910.

The young Cameron began to develop a fascination with politics, particularly Conservative politics. One contemporary remembers Cameron, at a weekend party, playing a game that involved listing past Tory Prime Ministers as far back as you could go.

'The first bit was easy – Major, Thatcher, Heath...' says the contemporary, 'but he could keep on going back: Baldwin, Bonar Law, Balfour... It was like he was casting round the room, seeing who else took these things seriously.'

'Cameron is clearly aware of his political background,' says the historian Hywel Williams, who worked alongside him as a special adviser to John Major's Cabinet. 'When the Conservatives lost the Newbury by-election in 1993, he said, "Oh no, that was my great-grandfather's seat."'

Growing up in Berkshire, with an older brother and two sisters, one older, one younger, Cameron had the quintessential, upper-middle-class, rural childhood.

If you were searching for any unusual element, you might find it in Ian Cameron's disability. Born with severe deformation from the knees downward, in later life Ian Cameron had both legs amputated. Before this, he was involved in every aspect of country pursuits without mentioning his disability once.

'Whinging wasn't on the menu,' says one family member about the effect of Ian Cameron's disability.

'His legs were about half the length they should have been; he only had seven toes,' says Cameron. 'In his generation, it was quite a stigma. His mother and his father decided not to have any children after him. So he was an only child. His answer was to play cricket, tennis ... riding. He was a great dancer, a great bon viveur.'

Cameron inherited his father's love of sport and is particularly competitive at tennis, hating to play with anyone who is not up to scratch, his wife excepted.

This fascination with the active life was apparent in our 2006 interview, when we took off in the helicopter for the ride home from the military base outside Hereford that belongs to 22 SAS regiment. 'I love this *Boys' Own* stuff,' said Cameron, as he devoured a history of the SAS he had been given by the regiment's commanding officer.

We were given tea in the officers' mess in a modern building decorated with oil paintings of all the SAS's great triumphs – from action in the Second World War, when the regiment was founded, right up until the 1990–91 Gulf War. Many of the regiment's members were absent from the base at the time, fighting undercover in Afghanistan and Iraq.

In one corner, a pair of new split-leather cowboy boots, trimmed with a great deal of shiny buckles and twirly fretwork, gleamed in their glass case. Beneath, a small metal tag read, 'Uday's Boots'. Uday Hussein, that is – Saddam Hussein's psychopathic oldest son, killed by allied special forces alongside his brother Qusay in Mosul in 2003.

Our tea was served by the adjutant of the camp, a trim man in military fatigues, his age given away only by his greying moustache.

'Milk and sugar?' he barked with military precision. 'Biscuit?' he added, proffering a plate of Jammie Dodgers.

'Quite incredible, that man,' said Cameron, as our helicopter took off from among a collection of camouflaged military helicopters. 'He fought in the Falklands and in the most recent war in Iraq. That's more than twenty years apart. It's like those soldiers who fought in the First and Second World Wars. Quite incredible. Must have been fighting in his early forties.'

His eyes grew wide with enthusiasm at the exploits of this veteran soldier.

Cameron's closeness to his family was reflected in his policies – those that favoured the family seemed the closest to his heart. When I first interviewed him – in 2006, at that centre in north Wales that allowed poor families to live together at low cost – he said, 'That is exactly how these things should be run. Don't get rid of government altogether, but let it take a back seat so that charities and individuals can take over. Families should not be controlled by the state.'

He is devoted to family life, too.

'We must be back by six,' Cameron said that day, as we prepared to fly off in a helicopter to Telford. 'I have not done bathtime for a bit.'

In a 2015 interview with Cameron, talk turned to the death of his son Ivan, in 2009.

'If you can get through that, you can get through anything,' said Cameron.

It takes over your life. We both worked out that we would cope, and find a way through this. He was a blessing in lots of

ways. But certainly, when he died, your whole world collaps-
es. You push pause on your life; you stop and have a think.
Nothing else really matters at that stage.

Friends say Ivan's disability had a huge effect on Cameron's
character, not least because it was the first knock in his
charmed life.

It is true, it is a knock. Having children changes you anyway
because you suddenly have to think about all the issues from
childcare to schooling, how you relate to the health service. It
changes your perspective on life. But having a disabled child
does particularly, because it's very tough. There are all sorts
of different things you need to sort out. You become a part-
time parent, nurse, carer, doctor. You are exhausted.

We weren't falling out with each other but we were falling apart, as in just coping with the nights and everything. I
always say to other people with disabled children, 'Remember, you're not an angel. You didn't volunteer for this. It happened to you. You've got to focus, as well as on your amazing
child, you've got to focus on yourself, your relationship and
keeping body and soul together. Because, if you fall apart,
they fall apart. You don't try to be something you're not. So,
recognise your shortcomings.'

Parents with perfectly healthy children, there are moments when we lose our temper with them, when we don't
do enough of their homework. The way to be a better parent
is to recognise your shortcomings.

Cameron talked freely about Ivan – not just to me, but to the envelope-stuffers in Cannock Conservative Club when we dropped in there in 2015. When one volunteer brought up Cherie Blair, Cameron reveals a soft spot for her. 'She was very good to Ivan, getting down to his level, showing him love.'

Even after he'd been in the job for years, it was still a bit of a shock to see your cousin in Downing Street. At family gatherings over the years, he was a million miles from the adolescent William Hague or Margaret Thatcher, the politician in embryo. He was never the teenage nerd, eyes fixed firmly on political power.

'I was only pretty moderate at school,' he says. 'I got a reasonable score to get into Eton. When I was sixteen, I was drifting; I was getting bored with it all. I didn't get particularly good O-level results.'

And then something peculiar happened. At sixteen – when some teenagers come off the rails – Cameron leapt onto them. Some contemporaries say that, previously, he felt in the shadow of his brother, Alexander, three years his senior and in the same house at Eton. More significantly, he started enjoying his economics and politics A-levels.

'I really loved what I was doing,' he says. 'I loved history of art, I'd always been passionate about history, and I'd enjoyed the economics and the politics. I suddenly thought, I love my subjects, and I was switched on.' So switched on that he confided in his mother about his love of politics.

'Mum said you must talk to Cousin Ferdy,' says Cameron. Cousin Ferdy is my father, Ferdinand Mount, head of

Thatcher's policy unit from 1982 to 1983. Mary Cameron rang Dad up, asking if the sixteen-year-old Dave could interview him for the school magazine. Dad said he was busy, and that he was restricted by the Official Secrets Act, but might be in touch. Moments later, Cameron rang up his office to book an appointment. He turned up at Downing Street, in Dad's words, 'looking pink and perky, not yet the size he grew to, but abounding in self-confidence'.

In his gap year, Cameron worked for his godfather, the Tory MP for Lewes, Tim Rathbone.

'I thought there's something extraordinarily satisfying about the work,' says Cameron.

> It is a vocation. And I think I found my vocation. I saw what he was doing and what others were doing – that mixture of public service and community service. I thought that was more interesting than anything else and that view hasn't really changed.
>
> I didn't think – therefore I want to be an MP. I thought that's interesting; maybe I could go and work in the House of Commons, be a researcher. I wasn't fixed on being an MP till later.

Cameron's Oxford contemporaries remember his confidence, although the writer Rachel Johnson, who was in the year above, says it was only in later life that he developed 'big-cocked confidence'. She means the term metaphorically, she hastens to add. Others say he was planning a political career even then. Cameron denies this.

But, certainly, that political interest was bubbling away at Oxford when Cameron saw an advert in the university careers department.

'I remember this quite clearly – "Conservative Research Department: bright graduates needed," he says. 'I thought, that looks interesting.

'And I remember applying, and going there and thinking, yes, I like this. Politics and issues. Felt like a good bridge into your first job. Something you were familiar with – researching, working, writing.'

At the CRD, he realised he wanted to be 'in the front room, not the back room'.

'I want to be serving a constituency, fixing problems, getting stuff done, rather than helping in the engine room,' he says. 'I enjoyed the engine room but I quite soon thought I'd like to get out … I learnt loads and worked with some very bright people.'

It was that time in the CRD that really explains Cameron's political character.

'People think Cameron and Boris are the same because of Eton, Oxford and the Bullingdon,' says Andrew Gimson. 'But Boris is really an anarchist, and Cameron is the ultimate insider. People bang on about the Bullingdon but a few drunken nights is nothing compared to years in the Conservative Research Department. He's the Establishment man writ large – he will always do what the Establishment thinks prudent.'

He was elected MP for Witney in 2001. Even then, he

wasn't desperate to become Prime Minister. 'In the 2001–05 parliament, there were a few of us who got together and talked about, gosh, what the Conservative Party had to do to get back into the centre ground to get back into contention,' he says. 'Danny Finkelstein, George Osborne, Michael Gove. There was no assumption that there was one torchbearer who was going to carry this project forward.'

As a Tory insider since 1988, when did Cameron realise that the Conservative message had to change?

'It wasn't an epiphany,' he says. 'It was a gradual thing. There were moments when I thought, this was wrong. But the real thinking happened when George sat down during the leadership campaign and thought it all out.'

As a fully coherent modernising programme, even at that early stage?

'Yes.'

The modernisation process had already begun under William Hague.

'William Hague did a great job,' says Cameron.

The Tory Party was in calamitous breakdown after '97 and he steadied the ship. William always said that he started in the direction of modernisation and he couldn't really sustain it because the party was in such a precarious position and it was so obvious Blair was going to get re-elected. And he had to just try and keep the show on the road. Which he did.

I always think what I did wouldn't have been possible without William Hague and then Michael Howard restoring a reputation for competence and professionalism and making sure the party got its act together.

There was a growing understanding that a number of things had to change. You had to address some things that were holding the Conservative Party back. Some were attitudes to gay people. In terms of not representing and reflecting modern Britain enough.

We didn't have enough women candidates for Parliament. We didn't reach out to enough ethnic minority voters who backed a lot of our values but didn't see themselves in the Conservative Party. We needed to spread ourselves across the country. We needed to address issues – the environment – as well as core values like defence, economy, foreign affairs.

So a whole set of things needed to change. What was useful about getting into the Commons in 2001 was time thinking and arguing and talking is rarely wasted in politics these days. People think that all politicians do is talk but sometimes there's no substitute for really going at things, thrashing it out, arguing.

And I was by no means the kind of fastest to the draw on what needed to change. I was influenced by what others thought. I listened a lot to Danny Finkelstein, Michael, George.

Michael particularly is a wonderful – I don't know if you can be an iconoclastic polemicist – but he's brilliant through the force of argument at smashing things down and building new things up. Making you think.

Cameron also acknowledges a debt to Tony Blair.

'Do you need to be an effective communicator in politics? Take people with you? Of course you do,' he says.

There's always more you can do on that front.

The biggest lesson we took from Blair was: use your time effectively. You're running a country, not a 24-hour news channel, as I once put it. Blair was still fighting the '97 election every day from '97 to 2001. He would admit that time was wasted.

'The pressure to respond to every news event is immense,' Cameron adds.

When I take people into the Cabinet Room, I say, this is one of the rooms where, for five days in May, Churchill and others decided that Britain should fight on against Hitler. Imagine if that happened today – after half an hour, Alastair Campbell or Craig Oliver [Cameron's director of communications] would pop his head round the door and say, 'Sky News are outside. What do I say? Are we fighting on or are we surrendering?' You've got to use your time to make long-term decisions for the good of the country. That was one of the biggest lessons I learnt from Blair.

I was determined to use your time to do the things that were necessary and to put into place the values you believe in and to serve your country. You can accuse this government of many things but time-wasting is not one of them. Fundamental reforms of education, welfare, deficit reduction, making it easier to invest in Britain, completely changing how the Foreign Office works, incentivise business and wealth creation. These are big, big changes.

Cameron's critics accuse him of being too beholden to opinion polls. Roughly half the people I talked to thought Cameron was the trimming PR man who sways with the wind; the other half thought him a gifted pragmatist whose enthusiasm and genial ability to compromise held the coalition together – a coalition which, by its nature, prevented him from delivering right-of-centre red meat.

'We made the coalition work and work quite well,' he says. 'It's held us back in some regards. But, in the main core task of turning the economy around, we went into coalition with a group of people who did realise that was the most important task facing the country.'

Cameron defined himself to me as a traditional Conservative with a rural upbringing. If you want to locate the roots of his Conservatism, look no further than his childhood home, the Old Rectory in Peasemore, Berkshire – one of the most naturally Conservative areas in the country. The WI and the church are strong; every village is an informal Tory branch. Here, where Conservatism is an undogmatic instinct rather than an ideology, is where Cameron, and his politics, were born.

'In many ways, I'm quite a traditional Conservative,' he says. 'I believe in family, community, country. I love Britain's great institutions. I think they should be preserved and enhanced. That's the best sort of conservatism – you take what is best out of your country and change the things that need to change.'

There are those who say Cameron is an empty vessel with no core set of ideas. When I put that to him in 2015, he bristled at the idea, and embarked on a long exegesis of what you might call Cameronism.

'The reason why people sometimes say that about me is I'm a cautious and practical person – and I think politics is about practicalities as well as about ideals,' he says.

I do have very strong ideals – about the opportunities I want people to have, people from every background, from every walk of life. What I say to my children about make the most of your talents is what I want for our country. With that comes a sense of fairness, not just that everyone gets a fair go, but also fair in that if you put in and make the effort, things should work out for you, rather than be held back.

I have very strong values, but I also believe politics is about duty, it's about action, it's about turning ideals into practice. The Conservative Party isn't much good as a party if it can't put its principles in action in government.

Duty is very important in politics. You don't choose when you get to become Prime Minister or necessarily what other job you do in government. The most important thing is to do the right thing. To do your duty. To act in a way that fits with what's right for the country and what you believe. That's sometimes overlooked.

I'm driven mad by people who say, why don't our politicians believe anything any more. Well, they do. We're driven by belief, by values.

Our government came along when Britain had a massive deficit, the economy wasn't growing. The most important duty at that point was to sort out the economy and turn it round. If you believe in public service, that's the service that the public required. You've got to damn well get on and do it. You can spend lots of time brushing up your ideas and principles, but you're not much bloody good if you don't fix the things that are broken.

Cameron is an odd combination: a clever, politically ambitious man inside an affable, uncomplicated skin. That relaxed affability explained his revelation before his second general election that he wouldn't fight a third as leader – a revelation that astounded many commentators, so used were they to politicians who wanted to fight on for ever. Friends said he and Sam loved living in Downing Street but understood it wasn't for ever.

That's why they weren't clinging to the front door like Gordon Brown, or in floods of tears, like Margaret Thatcher, when their time was up.

I could see how much Cameron enjoyed being Prime Minister in the spring of 2015, when I shadowed him on a trip to Saga's office in Hastings with Amber Rudd, then the local MP, now Home Secretary.

On the way back through Hastings train station, I walked

behind Cameron as he passed a pair of tracksuited teenagers, a boy and a girl, munching chips.

When he walked by, they both stopped munching and the boy said, open-mouthed, 'Bloody hell!'

Cameron saw them and – rather than being annoyed – said in a fruity, Leslie Phillips way, 'Hello!', enjoying their surprise, and intensifying it.

One political insider told me Cameron doesn't like being disagreed with; that no one stands up to him in Conservative inner circles except George Osborne. His aides denied this and he was happy to answer my questions, however critical, except for one. Why did he join the Bullingdon? I confessed to joining the club because my friends were in it.

'It's cripplingly embarrassing when you look back at those pictures now,' he says. 'I think I've said all I want to say about that.'

His reluctance contrasts with fellow Bullingdon member Boris Johnson, who deploys an ejector seat from class embarrassment by lampooning the whole thing. I've been greeted at parties by Boris bellowing, 'Buller! Buller! Buller!'

Cameron denies there's been a fight for political power with Boris since Eton. 'It would make a great book, but it's not true at all,' he says.

I remember Boris at school because he was so striking. He was dishevelled. I remember watching him play rugby. He was ferocious. Built like a second row.

I knew him a bit then; a little bit at university. Probably

got to know him better since. He was closer to my brother's year than to me. He was also in College – you knew people in College in your own year; but you didn't always know people in College in the years above you.

Any rivalry between them disappeared some time after Cameron became Prime Minister, he says.

He suddenly realised I'm not really his competition. His competition is people who'll have a crack at it after me. And [between us] I look at it as 'co-opetition'. I wanted him to stand for London mayor. George and I helped persuade him to do that. And he's done it brilliantly. A Conservative is running the most successful city on earth, and is winning elections.

Along with Cameron's confidence comes that old bugbear, class – an eternal gift to political cartoonists, who like dressing him in Eton tails or that Bullingdon outfit. On the day we travelled to Birmingham, Peter Brookes, in *The Times*, had drawn a cartoon of Cameron in tails, shouting 'Fag!' at Nick Clegg, who's floating in mid-air smoking a joint. 'They do make me laugh,' says Cameron. 'The meaner they are, the more they make you laugh.'

Cameron once confronted Steve Bell, the *Guardian* cartoonist, in a service station. Bell liked to depict Cameron with a condom over his head.

'I said, "What's all that about?"' says Cameron, 'And he said, "Your skin's so smooth." We had a very funny conversation, roaring with laughter in the car park, somewhere on the M6.'

The class attacks don't get him down. 'In the end, people make a judgement about whether you can do the job or not. That's what matters,' he says. 'You are who you are. I've never tried to hide who I am, or my background, or my schooling, or my parents. I haven't changed the way I speak; that's crazy.'

Professor Henry Higgins would have a field day with Cameron. He speaks with clipped vowels, but without braying, so his voice comes across as upmarket but not aggressively so. Income is 'incerm'; counties 'countuhs'; university 'universitih'.

Much has been made of Cameron's class over the years.

'William Hague found it incredibly frustrating,' says Cameron.

Here was a comprehensively educated boy from South Yorkshire. People assumed he was some sort of public-school toff. If you were completely out of touch with issues, problems, that would be bad.

People think you lead some rarefied existence as a PM but you don't, actually. You're out and about all the time, and you're a Member of Parliament, and you're a dad, and all those things.

If there was one thing that sparked off the class war attacks on Cameron, it was a particular Oxford club. Once a mainstay of cartoons and comment pieces, it has slipped back into the sleepy, champagne-fuelled oblivion from which it briefly emerged when Cameron became Tory leader in 2005.

CHAPTER 15

RIP THE BULLINGDON

My favourite conspiracy theory about the Bullingdon Club appears on a website called Abel Danger. The website claims:

> The Bullingdon Club at Oxford University recruits its members from the upper circles of society. Members' participation in acts of violence, sabotage, sex, S&M, drug use and other acts is filmed or otherwise recorded.
>
> Members are later placed in positions of power and influence throughout the world and controlled and blackmailed into executing the plans of the power behind the club – the House of Rothschild…
>
> Our research suggests that Rothschild investors used the Bullingdon hub to trigger insider trading frauds on the London Stock Exchange after the Battle of Waterloo (1815) and used the Bullingdon spokes, including former Fulbright scholar Barack Obama, to trigger insider trading frauds on the New York and the Chicago Stock Exchanges after the attack of 9/11.

Sadly, despite having been in the Bullingdon – and, by extension, the Bullingdon hub – from 1991 to 1993, I'm still awaiting the call placing me in a position of power and influence throughout the world. It's true that Nat Rothschild was in the club at the same time as me. When I've occasionally bumped into him, he is perfectly nice – but he's yet to get round to controlling and blackmailing me.

And it's also, sadly, untrue that the Buller has prepared me for world domination.

If the club was really such an effective powerbroker, it wouldn't have gone into such a steep decline. In 2016, it was reported that the Bullingdon was down to its last two members. That's barely enough people to trash each other's bedrooms, let alone a whole restaurant, as the Bullingdon is wont to do, according to legend – not that we ever did in my time.

Still, for the years of David Cameron's leadership of the Conservative Party – 2005–16 – the Bullingdon exerted a totemic power. The pictures of Cameron, Boris Johnson and George Osborne in those silly outfits ended up as their defining images – and led to all those mad conspiracy theories. The *Mail on Sunday* journalist Peter Hitchens was so convinced that the Bullingdon was full of political secrets that he thought a member had been airbrushed out of one photo. In fact, the photo, badly reproduced in a magazine, just showed the ghost of a member's white shirt accidentally transplanted to the opposite side of the picture.

'Remember, I saw this sort of doctoring the whole time in Communist Russia,' Hitchens told me gravely.

Rather than advancing an MP's career, the Bullingdon is pure Kryptonite for political ambition. It's not only the most famous university club in the world – it's also the most shameful.

In 1975, Tony Blair was photographed in a St John's College dining club while he was at Oxford. In the picture, he's wearing a boater and making a 'wanker' sign. But his reputation escaped largely unscathed, because the Archery Club is unknown, and because he wasn't thought of as posh in the first place. With Cameron an Old Etonian, and the Bullingdon so grand, that photograph went nuclear.

Cameron was certainly clubbable at Oxford – in 1987, he was president of the Gridiron, another university social club – where he had been less so at Eton.

'He didn't get into Pop [Eton's club of the most popular boys] because he so wanted to get in,' says one of his old teachers at Eton. 'I think that's why he was so keen to get into the Bullingdon.'

It makes sense, then, that the Bullingdon is largely made up of the ambitious – like David Cameron – rather than the dissolute. James Delingpole was right about the Bullingdon in *The Spectator* in August 2016, when he said of George Osborne:

Seduced by high-level shindigs at Davos, Brussels and wherever Bilderberg is holding its roadshow this year, [senior politicians] become convinced that the people best placed to run the world are a Brioni-suited cabal of enlightened corporatists, globalist technocrats and Goldman Sachs-trained central bankers like his Canadian import Mark Carney. It's like the Bullingdon for grown-ups, and naturally George wanted to be with them on the superyacht.

For all its modern fame, the Bullingdon was really rather ob-scure by the time I joined it in the early '90s. My friend Sam Leith, literary editor of *The Spectator*, who came up to my college, Magdalen, in the year I left, 1993, said he had never heard of the club in his three years at Oxford, despite being an Old Etonian.

I can understand why. The club wasn't secret – but it was cloaked in a veil of mild embarrassment. Even at the time, I felt somewhat ashamed of having joined the club. It was a silly thing to join – even at an age when people do silly things, and don't calculate how their behaviour will play in several decades' time.

I remember walking from Magdalen for the annual Bullingdon photograph. I skulked along Merton Street, hug-ging the rough limestone wall beside the pavement, my navy blue tailcoat and English mustard waistcoat bundled under my arm, to avoid embarrassment.

Members like Cameron, Osborne and Johnson didn't find their way to power because of the club. If anything, they made it to the top despite the deep embarrassment caused by pictures of them in those swanky tailcoats and studied poses. The simple fact is that the desire of clever, well-educated, ambitious men to join a supposedly exclusive club sometimes overlaps with the desire to be voted into Parliament. Bullingdon membership is no key to political success. It is a sign of a desire for popularity and an ambition to be voted into clubs, whether it's a university drinking club or the House of Commons.

Or to be voted into foreign parliaments, in fact. Radek Sikorski, the former Polish Foreign Minister, was in the Bullingdon with Cameron and Johnson. He wasn't a rich undergraduate, but he shared that desire for election to a supposed elite.

It's understandable that the media spotlight repeatedly zeroed in on those awkward photographs of the Bullingdon Club. But, in fact, the Bullingdon didn't loom very large in members' lives. It meets only twice a year: once for the dinner in the summer, when those silly photographs are taken; once for a spring breakfast and point-to-point in the Oxfordshire countryside.

The club takes its name from the old Bullingdon hundred, a chunk of Oxfordshire, south-east of Oxford – where that point-to-point was held. Until 1879, Bullingdon Green – now built over – was a cricket pitch on the outskirts of Oxford, between Horspath and Cowley. In the last recorded match on the pitch, the Bullingdon Club played I Zingari, the roving English cricket club with no fixed home.

The Bullingdon Craft and Social Club – an over-60s club – still meets every month in the Bullingdon Community Centre in Headington, on the outskirts of Oxford. It only changed its name from the Friendly Craft and Social Club to the Bullingdon Craft and Social Club in 2016. The shameful connotations of the other Bullingdon Club can't be that overpowering.

Another memory of the Bullingdon hundred is the Bullingdon pub, on Cowley Road in Oxford – now a cocktail bar and live music venue. Recent acts include Plaid, Gazelle Twin and Part Chimp – no, they aren't the surnames of old Buller members.

The only other major institution to take its name from the Bullingdon hundred is – appropriately enough, given the antics of some club members, like former jailbird Darius Guppy – Bullingdon Prison, a category B/C prison in Arncott, Oxfordshire. Famous inmates include Rolf Harris.

Given that most members weren't elected until the end of their first or second year, the average undergraduate member only went to four or five Bullingdon gatherings. The influence of those brief meetings on modern British politics would be a tiny footnote in history – but for those fatally ridiculous photographs. Mere snapshots in young lives have been blown up to mammoth, career-defining proportions.

Until the Cameron–Osborne–Johnson years, the Bullingdon was hardly a politician factory. In fact, even in those years, 90 per cent of the members ended up in normal professional careers – as bankers, businessmen, art historians and journalists.

For several centuries, the Bullingdon had been a sporting club, with some heavy drinking on the side. It began life as a hunting and cricket club in 1780 – the club badge still shows a cricket bat, stumps and a man on a horse.

The Bullingdon cricket team even played against the MCC. In 1795, the Buller lost by eight wickets at their cricket ground on Bullingdon Green; in the return fixture at Lord's, the MCC won by an innings and 382 runs. In 1796, the Bullingdon was again thumped, home and away, by the MCC. The MCC won yet again, at Lord's, in 1819 and 1820.

It was at the annual Bullingdon point-to-point in the 1920s that the late Lord Longford, a member, is said to have converted from Conservative to Labour. He fell off his horse, bumped his head, remounted and started riding in the opposite direction around the course. And so began his lifelong devotion to Labour politics.

The Bullingdon can behave appallingly – not least in 1894, when members smashed all 468 windows in Christ Church College's Peckwater Quad, and in 1927, when they did it all over again. As a punishment, the club was banned from meeting within fifteen miles of Oxford.

When the future Edward VIII, an undergraduate at Magdalen College just before the First World War, wanted to join the club, his mother, Queen Mary, was horrified. She let him do so only if he promised not to take part in a 'Bullingdon blind' – a drunken club dinner.

In his characteristic, authority-defying way, the Prince of Wales attended a 'blind' anyway, prompting a furious Queen Mary to send a telegram asking him to leave the club. An impossible request, I fear – even from a queen. As far as I understand the unwritten rules of the club, once a member, always a member. The only way out of the dark blue tailcoat is in a wooden box.

The club assumed a darker air under the ruthlessly satirical eye of Evelyn Waugh. In *Decline and Fall*, written in 1928, it is lampooned as the brutally destructive Bollinger Club – named after the champagne house.

At one Bollinger dinner, Waugh wrote, 'a fox had been brought in in a cage and stoned to death with champagne bottles'.

Bollinger members included 'epileptic royalty from their villas of exile; uncouth peers from crumbling country seats; smooth young men of uncertain tastes from embassies and legations; illiterate lairds from wet granite hovels in the Highlands; ambitious young barristers and Conservative candidates'.

At another dinner, the club 'broke up Mr Austen's grand piano, and stamped Lord Rending's cigars into his carpet, and smashed his china, and tore up Mr Partridge's sheets, and threw the Matisse into his lavatory'.

Labour politician Tom Driberg said this description was a 'mild account of the night of any Bullingdon Club dinner in Christ Church. Such a profusion of glass I never saw until the height of the Blitz. On such nights, any undergraduate who was believed to have "artistic" talents was an automatic target'.

In *Brideshead Revisited*, Waugh again attacked the Bullingdon (this time, by its real name) for attempting to dunk one of those artistic undergraduates, the camp Anthony Blanche, in Mercury – the fountain in Christ Church's biggest quad, with a statue of Mercury at its centre. The members, Waugh writes, were dressed 'like a lot of most disorderly footmen'. Blanche's reaction to the thuggish Bullingdon members is inspired:

> I got into the fountain and, you know, it really was most re-freshing, so I sported there a little and struck some attitudes, until they turned about and walked sulkily home, and I heard Boy Mulcaster saying, 'Anyway, we did put him in Mercury.' You know, Charles, that is just what they'll be saying in thirty years' time. When they're all married to scraggy little women like hens and have cretinous porcine sons like themselves getting drunk at the same club dinner in the same coloured coats, they'll still say when my name is mentioned, 'We put him in Mercury one night,' and their barnyard daughters will snigger and think their father was quite a dog in his day, and what a pity he's grown so dull. Oh, la fatigue du Nord!

But, if the club's appearances in modern literature are prominent, its influence on the Establishment is massively exaggerated. What is true is that modern politics is largely run not by Bullingdon members – certainly not any more it isn't, anyway – but by a marginally broader group of public schoolboys and Oxbridge graduates, among them Theresa May, who got a Second in Geography at St Hugh's College, Oxford, in 1977.

And that's not just the case with the Conservative Party. Nick Clegg went to Westminster School, Robinson College, Cambridge, and Minnesota University; Ed Miliband to Corpus Christi, Oxford, and the London School of Economics.

It says something for the elite nature of modern politics that even the maverick man of the people, Nigel Farage, went to a leading private school, Dulwich College, and worked in the City.

Still, it remains extraordinary that three powerful people in the period from 2010 to 2016 – the Prime Minister, the Chancellor of the Exchequer and the Mayor of London – were all in the same Oxford club, albeit at different times.

That single fact sheds a dazzling shaft of light on how the modern British Establishment works. What is true about the modern Establishment is as true now as it was a century ago. People who are comfortably off, well-educated, confident, clever, ambitious, popular in their own circle and keen to join select societies have a good chance of getting on in politics – and British life, generally.

These days, the comfortably off bit is particularly important. Politics is now so badly paid in comparison with other graduate careers, like banking and law, that rich graduates are better placed to choose the interesting but badly paid jobs that lead to powerful political positions. To a certain extent, the Bullingdon has always produced politicians – among them Alan Clark, Lord Lyell (Margaret Thatcher's solicitor general and John Major's attorney general) and Lord

Longford. But no previous Bullingdon member has got as far in politics as Cameron, Osborne and Johnson.

That's partly just the luck of the draw. But it's also because the route to political power and professional success has been eased for the privately educated in the past half-century or so.

It's no coincidence that the new Bullingdon generation came of age immediately after the mass destruction of grammar schools. Where are all today's Margaret Thatchers, Ted Heaths, Harold Wilsons and John Majors? They have mostly been denied the education that propelled their predecessors to the top of politics.

What being in the Bullingdon also meant was you had a few quid, or your family had a few quid. And that bled into grown-up life, when family money allowed both Cameron and Osborne to work for the peanuts wages of the Conservative Research Department, rather than the hedge fund and law office millions many of their contemporaries went for.

The new Bullingdon generation also came of age when politics became a swots' game. Cameron is the first Tory Prime Minister to get a First at Oxford since Harold Macmillan. Osborne was a Demy – or scholar – at Magdalen College, Oxford. Boris was a Brackenbury Scholar at Balliol, the brainiacs' Oxford college.

The Bullingdon, with all its silly clothes and poses, is a powerful symbol of modern politics. But it is a smokescreen masking the truth. Politics today – in all the main parties – is the preserve not of Bullingdon members, but of a slightly wider group: of well-educated, well-off Oxbridge graduates and public schoolboys.

Theresa May is trying to differentiate herself from the Bullingdon boys that preceded her, not least in her opening speech on the steps of Downing Street – when she proclaimed that she was on the side of the 'just managing', not 'a privileged few'. But, really, she isn't that different. Not only is she an Oxbridge graduate; she was also privately educated.

She emphasises her time at Holton Park Girls' Grammar School in Wheatley, Oxfordshire, which became Wheatley Park Comprehensive while she was there. But she also went to St Juliana's Convent School for Girls, a Catholic private school.

So, one privately educated Oxford graduate has, shock horror, been replaced by another privately educated Oxford graduate. But, still, thank God, one who isn't locked into the nefarious Bullingdon hub of global domination.

HOW THE REFERENDUM WAS LOST – AND WON

The make-up lady at the BBC's Millbank studio in Westminster has noticed a change in Boris Johnson's look.

'His hair is much smarter now,' she told me as she slapped anti-shine talc on my gleaming pate for the *Daily Politics* show. 'But he still messes it up a bit after I've combed it.'

Boris Mark II has entered the fray. As his conference speech in October 2016 showed, he's still making the gags but they now play second fiddle to his more serious aspirations – as a successful Foreign Secretary and, ultimately, Prime Minister.

Like some rare species of blond cockroach, Boris survived the post-referendum nuclear fallout, while the other Bullingdon boys and the Notting Hill Set were wiped off the face of the earth.

Even though he fought for Brexit, he was astonished at the aftermath – just look at his face, and Michael Gove's, in that press conference on 24 June, after David Cameron resigned.

Boris – normally so good at hiding his real feelings beneath a thousand onion skins – was shell-shocked.

Insiders say he was amazed to be offered the Foreign Secretary's job. His future seemed to offer little more than a backbencher's life, well-padded with the money from his *Telegraph* column, his books and a few celeb outings. The boy who said he wanted to be 'world king' when he grew up was destined to become little more than an upmarket Ed Balls, dismally touring the TV studios, living off the crumbs of yesteryear's fame.

For some time after he became Foreign Secretary in July, he went into comic purdah, as he jettisoned the clown costume. Craig Brown warned that 'Boris's chosen destiny is to become a sort of blond Jack Straw, flying all over the world to read boring speeches to bored audiences. Any possibility of offence or excitement will have been expertly excised, leaving nothing but a prolonged drone of unimpeachable waffle.'

That was certainly the case for a few months. But his Tory conference speech – in Birmingham in October 2016 – showed Funny Boris has taken over once again from Shocked Boris.

Welcome back, the lovely P. G. Wodehousian similes: asking people whether they were in favour of democracy is 'a bit like asking Maria von Trapp whether she was in favour of raindrops on roses and whiskers on kittens'.

Here again were the bathetic comparisons: 'Political freedom went with economic freedom like buying a two-for-one ice cream Snickers bar – only free markets could produce something so ingenious – and a copy of *Private Eye* – free speech of a kind still unknown in much of the planet.'

Boris also returned to his bewitching habit of raiding the dictionary and minting his own vocab. Here he was, enjoying 'vast and ruminative feasts of lunch or dinner in the castles of Mitteleuropa', having 'wonderful conversations in my various euro-creoles', taking on the 'lingering gloomadon-poppers'.

So, Comic Boris has returned. But, this time, there is a subtle shift. The jokes are no longer the main course: they are the hors d'oeuvres before the meaty entrée. His conference jokes were gaffe-free and uncontroversial, and the serious message beneath rang out loud and clear: that liberal democracy and British soft power are forces beyond compare.

Now Boris no longer has his *Telegraph* column, he doesn't have to pull in readers with the histrionic touches or OTT lines that were then turned by the press into gaffes.

Will the new-found seriousness take him all the way to No. 10? Who knows?

Either way, he has become the Great Survivor, while all the other Tory big beasts were shot down – ultimately because they backed the wrong horse.

Why did Remain – and the Tory high command of Cameron and Osborne – lose?

It was partly because they had failed to see how Eurosceptic Britain was – although both Osborne and Gove warned Cameron from the beginning that he might lose a referendum; that it would destroy the leading members of the government.

Osborne had always been a Europhile since his first days in

Conservative Central Office, shortly after leaving Oxford in 1993, after a brief spell in journalism.

'The very first conversation I had with George Osborne was '93/'94,' says Douglas Carswell.

> He was working in the Conservative Research Department. He spent dinner trying to convince me why we shouldn't rule out joining the euro.
>
> It made quite an impression on me. How on earth does one become a member of the CRD if you're planning to rule out your national currency? And then I realised that, in order to become a member of the CRD then, you had to have malleable opinions.

There was a problem with the finances of the Remain campaign, too. A Conservative activist told me:

> Lord Feldman [the Conservative Party deputy treasurer and chief fundraiser] didn't get the hot money [money freshly made by individual entrepreneurs]. People who'd made the money were more likely to leave. Remain relied on corporate donors and they were tainted by association with bankers such as Goldman Sachs, at a time when bankers aren't flavour of the month. It looked like 'Bankers for Remain'. Companies shouldn't tell people how to vote.

Because a Brexit vote was considered unfashionable, if not racist, a lot of the ABC voters kept their decision quiet, too.

'A lot of bankers were publicly in; privately out,' said the Conservative activist.

The Remain campaign also remained fundamentally London-based.

'It was a London campaign with London pollsters,' the Conservative activist said. 'They were working in an echo chamber, buttressing each other's opinions that they were going to win.'

So, there was a form of Leave guilt – just like Tory guilt, a concept which pollsters often account for at general elections by adding on a few per cent to the Conservative vote. No pollster accounted for Leave guilt. If anything, they went the other way.

The accuracy of the polls also depended on how they were done.

'Online polling tends to use cash incentives, and so attracts people on a lower income,' says Chris Bruni-Lowe, Nigel Farage's campaign director and chief pollster.

> It naturally favours the Leave side. YouGov, which does internet polling, tried to counter that and went too far the other way.
>
> Phone polling is much more accurate. Telephone polling on the day showed Leave ahead by 52 to 48. Survation and ICM are the only ones who do phone polling, and they were that much more accurate.

Dominic Cummings, in charge of the polling at Vote Leave, points out that, because so few of us answer our landlines, phone polling has become much more difficult.

'Because they can't get through on home phone lines, the margin of error is now 5, 6, 7 per cent, not 3 per cent,' he says.

A decade ago, half the people answered the phone. Now, it's one in twenty on home phone lines.

You can get mobile numbers, but you don't know the demographics of mobiles. On a landline, you have a postcode, which is predictive in all sorts of ways.

The whole science only works if your sample is random. Now they're not and they don't know in what direction they're not random.

The other thing that polls are bad at is tracking down the people who say they aren't going to vote, but, in the end, do.

'Why were the polls so hopelessly wrong for the referendum?' says Nigel Farage. 'They didn't read the non-voters. It's all well and good for YouGov to have a 1,000-voter tracker poll to see who's going in or out. But, if you haven't got the person who hangs the phone up when you ring, because he thinks you're a wanker...'

Farage breaks down into a series of trademark, tobacco-coated laughs. But the implication is clear. Remain didn't get the polls right – or get the victory – because they didn't go across the country and track down the quiet Brexiteers.

'You get them by going to where they live and where they drink and where they bet and where they watch football,' says Farage. 'It's not actually very hard because the local media are desperate for it. No one does this any more. Look at the

George Osborne style of politics: wear a hard hat and visit a factory. It's not very interesting, is it?'

If the pollsters got it wrong in the European referendum, they got it even more spectacularly wrong with the American election.

'The pundits and the punters got it wrong because they were talking to other people like them,' says Daniel Hannan. 'They found it difficult to imagine he could win. There must have been a shy Trump factor, too – in the same way, we're returning, post-crash, to an element of shy Tories over here.'

There's been a widespread suggestion that Brexit was caused by the same forces that caused Trump's victory, as well as Matteo Renzi's referendum defeat in Italy on 4 December 2016.

'There's a huge difference between the Leave win and the Trump win,' says Daniel Hannan.

The Leave campaign wasn't nativist or protectionist. If it had been an anti-modern, anti-foreigner campaign, it wouldn't have got into double figures, let alone won.

A big part of Trump's schtick is that he doesn't want a free-trade deal with China. A big part of ours was that we did want one. The parallel doesn't work, except in one narrow sense. In both cases, there was an anger at remote elites.

Farage and UKIP were closer to Trump in their message, but they accounted for a small chunk of people, whose votes weren't ever really in doubt.

As on so many questions, there is a fundamental difference of opinion between leading members of Vote Leave and Leave.EU about the Brexit parallels with Trump.

'The American crossover with Brexit is extraordinary,' says Nigel Farage, speaking in December 2016.

> I've felt it since I went over to Mississippi in August, and in the five times I've been over since then.
>
> We had similar mood music and even the slogans were similar – 'Make America Great Again' and what was UKIP's? 'Believe in Britain.'
>
> Even the policy areas are similar. Trump is keen on free trade. He wants free trade with countries of equivalence – like the UK. Only when there are countries with different environmental standards – like China – then it's not fair.

The question still remains: why did Leave win? There's a good argument for saying that they were always going to – and that all the argy-bargy made little difference.

'Dom [Cummings] said in January that Leave would win 52–48,' says Cleo Watson, Vote Leave's head of outreach.

'I was always optimistic,' says Douglas Carswell. 'I consistently said it would be 53–47. I said that two weeks before polling data showing a wider margin.'

'"This is for us to lose," I said to Matthew Elliott right at the beginning of the campaign,' says Sir Bill Cash, the Eurosceptic MP.

We had some pretty harrowing moments – and there were people working incredibly long hours, doing an enormous amount of work. It was nationwide, far bigger than AV ever was, or the Scottish referendum.

But, ultimately, the people made their own decisions. And I always believed the British people would make the right decision – and they did.

In many areas of the country, MPs ran their own personal campaigns to leave the EU, which were distinctly different from the Vote Leave campaign itself, with correspondingly strong results.

Still, it's worth remembering that it was a close-run thing in the end, with victory by 17.4 million to 16.1 million. It was by no means a racing certainty.

Undeniably, the Vote Leave team worked at a Stakhanovite rate to tip the odds in their favour.

'You were in by seven. From March, it was weekends, too. It was gruelling,' says Cleo Watson. 'Everyone got really fat and there was borderline alcoholism going on.'

And, whatever the truth of the Farage Paradox, it's certainly true that Farage did bolster votes in his own natural heartland.

'We didn't get everything right,' Farage says,

but we had at least done our homework a year before and knew roughly where we wanted to go. I regretted bitterly that all the different groups didn't get together under a big, broad umbrella, and yet, looking back at it now, maybe it was for the best.

We all did our own thing. Once the Labour Party had given up with Vote Leave, they were doing their own thing. They may have been a small team but they were very effective, with Kate Hoey and John Mills and that secretariat. They were reaching out to a bit of a community.

We had Banks firing out with Leave.EU. Maybe, in the end, independent flowers blooming wasn't such a bad thing. It wasn't the way I wanted it to be.

Senior Tories on the Remain side certainly don't believe in the Farage Paradox.

'They won, didn't they?' says one of George Osborne's senior advisers.

And Vote Leave didn't keep immigration quiet. Look at the posters they put out about Turkey joining the EU.

Yes, they were a coalition of all sorts of interests. But it was a small number of people who voted for more trade, who wanted a Singapore-on-Thames as a result of Brexit. But that was a small subset of the London elite. It amuses me, people, after the event, saying voters weren't voting against immigration. Of course they were. Educational qualification was the biggest driver. The Remain vote was highest among those with degrees.

If immigration was key to many Leave voters – as Osborne's adviser claims – then Tony Blair was the man who was responsible for immigration on an unprecedented scale: partly, Jack Straw admitted, because it would shore up the Labour vote; partly because Labour saw immigration as a good in and of itself.

Conservative Prime Ministers did little to deal with the issue. Theresa May regularly made tough suggestions to tackle the immigration issue during the coalition government of 2010–15; and Nick Clegg regularly vetoed them. And even those targets that were accepted weren't met during May's tenure at the Home Office – as she confirmed in her Lancaster House speech in January 2017, saying: 'As Home Secretary for six years, I know that you cannot control immigration overall when there is free movement to Britain from Europe.'

In the end, voters heard what they wanted to hear. Those who were anti-immigration listened to Nigel Farage. Those who wanted to leave on sovereignty grounds listened to Vote Leave.

'All countries have their share of people who are inward-looking, Britain less than most,' says Daniel Hannan.

Those weren't the people Vote Leave targeted in its messages, in its iconography. The thing that's overlooked is that, in every debate, Gove and Boris and Gisela all wanted immigration. Boris, in the final debate, asked for an amnesty for illegal immigrants. It wasn't something we were trying to slip out in the small print. Remain didn't hear it because it didn't fit their caricature of us.

It also helped the Leave cause that successive Prime Ministers had grown too comfortable in the European club to set about reforming it. All the while, the groundswell of Euro-sceptic opinion was growing. To be fair to David Cameron, there is a good argument for saying that, if he hadn't put the issue to the vote, one of his successors would have. Britain is a majority Eurosceptic country, albeit by a small margin.

'In the polling we did at the beginning of the campaign, a third of people were strongly Eurosceptic, another third wanted to leave the EU but were worried about the effects on their jobs, and another third were strongly Europhile,' says one Vote Leave analyst.

Throw in the effects of the euro crisis in southern Europe, the migrant crisis and Cameron's failure to get a proper deal from the EU – and you begin to see why the result ended up as it did.

That natural Euroscepticism of the British has been snow-balling in recent years, too. At the 2014 European elections, UKIP was the majority party – with twenty-four seats to Labour's twenty and the Tories' nineteen, and the Lib Dems' one seat. It's easy to forget quite what a recent phenomenon such massive UKIP success is.

'In 2005, we got one mention a week in the press; two, if we were lucky,' says Gawain Towler, UKIP's press secretary.

Yes, many natural Tories voted UKIP for tactical reasons in those 2014 European elections – but they did that because they felt strongly about Europe, and wanted to show the Tories how strongly they felt. They were the same voters who moved back to the Tories at the 2015 election, and gave David Cameron a majority – but that didn't mean they'd stopped being naturally Eurosceptic.

It's striking, too, that the vast majority of the House of Commons were for Remain – i.e. they were out of kilter with the population at large. With the benefit of hindsight, that presents David Cameron with a conundrum. Might he have survived without a referendum? The majority of MPs in the House would have been with him. But would those UKIP voters of the 2014 European referendum who came over to him in the 2015 general election have done so without his promise of a referendum if he won a majority? It is impossible to know.

Cameron might well have won in 2015 without the promise of a referendum. But that disconnect – between a huge Eurosceptic constituency in the country and a largely Europhile Parliament – wouldn't have gone away. Like Margaret Thatcher and John Major, he might have been toppled by the Eurosceptics in the end; and, if not him, his successor.

But any Europhile Prime Minister taking the Eurosceptic bull by the horns would have had to defend his corner robustly. With hindsight, Cameron and Osborne were wrong to run a negative campaign in Project Fear – even if, as Osborne's adviser says, they began on a positive front before turning negative. They also should have picked up on that disconnect between a largely pro-EU Parliament and a marginally anti-EU population. So, they shouldn't have had a referendum and – if they did – they should have sung the EU's praises.

That disconnect was symptomatic of a more general phenomenon during the referendum: the more powerful you were, the more Europhile you became. It was, admittedly, more an English phenomenon than a Scottish or a Northern

Irish one. But, still, according to Lord Ashcroft's polling in September 2016, the only income group to vote Remain by a majority was in households with an annual income of more than £60,000. Nigel Farage noticed a similar phenomenon in the Trump victory.

'America isn't working for ordinary people,' he says. 'It's great if you're rich.'

I saw the phenomenon writ large at a swanky party in Bond Street, central London, held on 14 April 2016, by the auction house Bonhams and the car maker Bentley. A Bentley, painted in pleasingly garish colours by the pop artist Sir Peter Blake, was being auctioned for charity.

Talking to a sophisticated-looking woman – fifties, elegant black dress, perfect bone structure – I admitted I was for Brexit. I didn't volunteer my opinion. I only admitted to my position when another person in the conversation asked me which way I was going to vote. I'd never met this woman before but, still, she went completely bonkers.

'How could you?' she shouted. 'Do you know what France will do to you if you get your way?'

I'm sure France doesn't hate me that much. Yet it wasn't France she was really worried about – it was the shock that anyone in such a glitzy setting could belong to the oiky, myopic world of Eurosceptic Little Englanders.

The other powerful factor was age. According to Lord Ashcroft's polls, 73 per cent of 18–24-year-olds voted Remain, falling to two thirds among 25–34s. A majority of over-45s voted to leave, rising to 60 per cent for over-65s.

This was an area where Matteo Renzi's referendum loss in Italy in December 2016 differed strongly from the European referendum result.

'Yes, there was an anti-establishment feeling there, too,' says Nigel Farage.

> But Beppe Grillo's movement [the Five Star Movement] is full of younger people in their thirties and forties. It was the old who went for the status quo.
>
> The difference was that the young had seen what a catastrophe the euro is, as well as taking against remote elites. If we'd joined the euro, a lot more young people would have voted for Brexit. They would have seen that Europe does not work.

The referendum had strong class, power and money aspects to it. Broadly speaking, the posher, more powerful and richer you are, the more Europhile you are.

'If you believe in the European project, you probably think the economic and social affairs are best organised by grand design,' says Douglas Carswell.

> Like a priest being exposed to grand design, it's profoundly threatening to your world view to hear otherwise. If you're in close proximity to the designer, you tend to be in favour of the blueprint.
>
> The rich, property-owning London elite have had their asset wealth massively inflated. The difference between the

asset rich and the wage wealth has opened up. Those who are rich because of asset inflation felt threatened by this [Brexit].

I had a hedge fund manager complain that this [Brexit] will cost him a fortune. Am I supposed to apologise for not arranging the country's affairs for him?

The grand Camerons were Europhile; Johnson (a less grand Etonian than Cameron), Gove and Vine Brexiteers. And rich, metropolitan London was more Europhile than the poorer, unfashionable provinces.

'In most organisations, people get more Europhile the higher up they are,' said Daniel Hannan. 'The NFU leadership are more Europhile than most farmers; the TUC leadership more Europhile than most manual workers; Church of England bishops more Europhile than their congregations.'

You see the same pattern in politics: the more powerful you are, the more Europhile. The Cabinet was largely in favour of remaining. Conservative backbenchers were split about 50–50. Among party members, the split was three to one in favour of leaving.

Class explained the actress Emma Thompson's Europhile attack on Britain, in February 2016, as 'a tiny little cloud-bolted, rainy corner of sort-of Europe, a cake-filled, misery-laden, grey, old island'. The implication was clear: if you're a sophisticated, upper-middle-class, Cambridge-educated, Oscar-winning type, then, naturally, you're all for staying in the cake-free sunlit uplands of Europe.

As Toby Young pointed out, the Cabinet split along class

lines. The Eurosceptics – Iain Duncan Smith, Chris Grayling and Priti Patel – were largely state-educated. The privately educated – Cameron, Osborne, Jeremy Hunt, Nicky Morgan and Amber Rudd – were mostly for Remain. Comprehensive-educated Young was a keen Brexiteer.

Class and power also explained the attack on Johnson by the banking grandee Sir Evelyn de Rothschild, in March 2016. Boris, Rothschild thundered, was 'a jack of all trades' who accumulated jobs like scout badges. 'If you want better terms of membership,' Rothschild said, 'you have to stay in the club.'

It's certainly true that people in the elite club were mostly Europhile – the megabanks, the CBI, the Foreign Office, the BBC, the civil service and Peter Mandelson among them.

If you were in the club, then, not surprisingly, you were rather keen on the status quo. And if you were in the club, like Sir Evelyn de Rothschild – or my glamorous new friend at the Bonhams–Bentley evening – you were astonished when a fellow club member, like Boris, turned traitor and resigned his membership.

In 1954, Nancy Mitford popularised the terms 'U' and 'non-U', as shorthand for upper-class and not upper-class. During the referendum campaign, opinions on the EU were just as divisive. How EU were you?

The split in opinion cut right through couples and families. During that last six weeks before the referendum, the tension between Remainers and Leavers swelled across the country. It's been centuries since a political issue so violently turned friend against friend, husband against wife and brother against sister.

David Cameron admitted he wasn't such good friends with Boris Johnson after the latter came out for Brexit. Samantha Cameron and Sarah Vine, Michael Gove's wife, once pals, are said to have had a stand-up row at a party over the referendum – and apparently haven't spoken to each other since.

Families, too, were sliced down the middle, not least Johnson's. His father, Stanley, a former Conservative MEP, was for staying in, as were Johnson's brother, Jo, the minister for universities and science, and sister, Rachel.

'The referendum campaign is far better at revealing political personality than anything else,' said Rachel Johnson at the time. 'There is right on both sides, so this debate doesn't just divide the country, party and family – it splits each voter down the middle too. Or it does in my family, anyway.'

That split was much wider than the usual political divide between friends and families at general election time. Because general elections come round every four or five years, we have a good idea of the political allegiances of our friends and family. But our European allegiances remain largely unexplored territory. And the European question is so broad that it grabbed people's hearts in utterly unpredictable ways.

When we air our hidden feelings for the first time, the sudden revelation can be explosive – even, or especially, within a marriage.

The writer A. N. Wilson wanted to stay in Europe because, he said,

The original idea of the Franco-German iron and steel agreement was a noble idea. It grew into the EEC, then the EU, and it has accomplished something we have never seen in the whole of European history since the end of the Roman Empire – namely peace between the lands now known as France and Germany. If we leave now, it will encourage all the really nasty elements in Europe.

Wilson's wife, Ruth Guilding, a writer and art historian, was a keen Brexiteer because, she said, 'Our union with Europe is like an abusive marriage in which freedom of choice has been traded for security – like Rob and Helen's in *The Archers*. And because change is always invigorating and staying means stagnation. And it is the patriot's choice.'

In the media, there was another divide, distinct from the class/wealth division: the split between the state-run, pro-EU BBC, and the largely Eurosceptic, privately owned newspapers.

'I turned down anything on *Newsnight* or the *Today* programme because I thought I'm going to lose my temper with you guys, because the producers and the editors and the presenters are just so out of touch,' says Douglas Carswell. 'The mainstream media pundits are part of this country's problem – they failed to analyse the problems.'

It didn't help that the Eurosceptics, despite their growing influence, were treated as nutjobs. In April 2006, David Cameron said, on LBC, 'UKIP is sort of a bunch of … fruitcakes and loonies and closet racists, mostly.'

'They always thought that people like Dan Hannan were slightly eccentric,' says Douglas Carswell.

It's very easy, when you're surrounded by ministerial boxes, with enormous patronage, with your flattering, urbane civil servants, to be contemptuously dismissive of Dominic Cummings and Dan Hannan. But, in this long march, they were right.

[Remainers] underestimated their opponents because they failed to understand the argument. To this day, many Remainers still think we're nativists who dislike the world. The tragedy is of their own making. If they'd understood Eurosceptics aren't backward-looking, aren't nativists, they're not reactionary, they're not Nigel [Farage].

The ruling elite in this country think they can organise affairs by their blueprint. They suffer from a neophilia.

And the EU, even after more than forty years, seemed like the new thing in Britain.

Carswell says, 'Blair exhibited this, saying, "We're a young country." Some Tories want to get down with the in crowd at Matthew Freud's parties. They fall for the new and the faddish.

'They should have been critical in assessing Europe policy, but weren't because they want to seem new and fashionable.'

Daniel Hannan used to say in *Telegraph* leader conferences that the internal contradictions of the EU were so great that it would eventually fall apart – it was just impossible to know when.

Nigel Farage agrees.

'I thought the whole thing would blow up before we had the courage to do anything about it,' he says.

Economic and monetary union doesn't work.

I didn't know when it would fall apart. If I'd known that, I'd have been down at Ladbrokes, not talking to you. I never knew. I started off, twenty-five years ago, [thinking] that we were a square peg in a round hole, that it didn't work [for Britain]. As the years went by, my view changed, that it doesn't work for anybody.

I used to think, if they want it south of Calais, let them have it. But now I think it's bad for the whole of Europe. There's going to be a different European debate across the whole of Europe, now we've got Brexit.

This growing dissatisfaction with Europe coincided with the rise of an increasingly prominent group of figures who organised the various Brexit campaigns. Even if one half of them hated the other half, I was struck by various similarities between them.

Daniel Hannan, Douglas Carswell, Michael Gove, Dominic Cummings and Nigel Farage are all extremely intelligent and eloquent. So intelligent and eloquent that they are almost odd in the ability to speak in complete paragraphs that can be written down as pure prose.

They are all public school-educated: Daniel Hannan (Marlborough), Douglas Carswell (St Andrew's School in

Kenya, and Charterhouse), Michael Gove (Robert Gordon's College, Aberdeen), Dominic Cummings (Durham School) and Nigel Farage (Dulwich College). Both Hannan and Cummings got Firsts in History from Oxford in the same year, 1994.

While Brexit voters were often wrongly classified as ignorant, northern and working class, there was a strong intellectual strain to the prominent Brexiteers.

That strain was on conspicuous display at the March 2016 launch of Hannan's book, *Why Vote Leave* – held in the Sky Bar at the top of Millbank Tower, near Parliament. Boris Johnson gave the big speech. He ended it with Hannan's line, '*Pactio Olisipiensis Censenda Est*', a take on Cato's repeated line in the Roman Senate: '*Carthago delenda est*' – 'Carthage must be destroyed.' Hannan's version means 'The Lisbon Treaty must be voted on.'

Despite their Establishment credentials, all the main Leavers were outsider–insiders. Their intelligence, independence of mind and loner tendencies mean they all see the world at a slight remove; that they can see the club, of the great and the good, with a half-cocked eye and a dose of cynicism.

It sounds ridiculous of such a successful public schoolboy but there was also an element of inverted snobbery to Nigel Farage. He referred mockingly to Old Etonians, as if he, an Old Alleynian, came from a different universe. 'We worked with anybody,' he said.

I even got George Galloway on a platform. Who else could

talk to the Muslim community? A bunch of Old Etonians – I'm sorry [Farage knows I am David Cameron's cousin] – are going to go and patronise them? Polling showed us that George still had a significant voice with the hard left. He may only be polling 1.4 per cent in the mayoral elections but at least he gets listened to in mosques in Bradford. Bradford voted to leave.

Farage also referred to Michael Gove and Boris Johnson as 'the snobs' – an odd term for Gove, the adopted son of an Aberdeen fish merchant, who attended Robert Gordon's College on a scholarship.

Even Boris Johnson, the lone Old Etonian among the Brexiteers, is an outsider–insider. A quarter Turkish, he comes from a family that is prominent but not as rich as you might think. He got a scholarship at Eton, meaning he become a Colleger, one of the planet-brained pupils who occupy a separate, most ancient part of the medieval school. Even in College, Boris was something of an outsider – he got an internal scholarship, meaning he applied for it once he was at the school, not before as most Collegers do. All his brothers got scholarships, too.

With this ragbag of independently minded, outspoken loners combining to push for Brexit, it's hard to point to any one individual who clinched it.

It's particularly hard in the world of politicians – who tend to think their individual efforts in their career make a greater contribution to the British political story than they in fact do. Retired politicians are always quick to bring up their minimal achievements early on in any conversation.

'I'm not sure if you're aware that I was once junior under-minister for paperclips in 1968,' they say. 'Had a tremendous impact.'

Most of the figures in the Brexit campaign also think it was their strategy that won the day; their polling that was right. UKIP thought Vote Leave was ineffectual; Vote Leave thought UKIP was toxic. They can't both be right. But they could both, separately, pull in different sorts of supporters, as well as appealing sometimes to the same ones.

Paradoxically, it helped, too, that the Leave groups were largely run on a shoestring. UKIP's principal team was eight-strong, in a Westminster terraced house; Vote Leave went up to 140 employees at its biggest, but for its first three months of operation barely employed more than ten people.

'They were a small group of people and they had the advantage of being a rebel force,' says a senior adviser to George Osborne. 'We had a much bigger group: Labour, Conservatives, the CBI, trade unions. We had breadth and we got on well with each other, but we weren't fleet of foot.'

In a funny way, even being short of cash helped Vote Leave.

'If we'd had lots of money, it would have been less stressful,' says Victoria Woodcock, director of operations at Vote Leave. 'We wouldn't have approached things in the way we did, which was clever and careful.'

In the end, the various Brexit campaigns never coalesced; they were often kept apart, in fact, by mutual loathing. But, by mistake, they ended up appealing to different constituencies, and worked accidentally to complement each other.

Nigel Farage, with his blaringly loud dog whistle on immigration, made a direct appeal to the hard right, the deindustrialised working class, the unemployed, and disenchanted working-class Labour voters.

Vote Leave appealed to the constitutional Brexiteers – the ones who'd had enough of their legislation being dictated by Europe. Boris Johnson gave Vote Leave the sheen of celebrity that allowed its reach to extend beyond the pointy-headed Eurosceptics.

Kate Hoey, Gisela Stuart and Frank Field removed the Conservative sting from the Brexit message. The suboptimal efforts of Jeremy Corbyn, too, helped Labour voters feel confident that a Brexit vote wasn't incompatible with voting Labour.

In the end, this bristling group of mutually loathing, staunchly independent groupuscules never unified over anything – except their desire to leave the EU. In that, they hit a strong chord of sympathy with a marginal majority of the British population.

And the rest was history.

ACKNOWLEDGEMENTS

I'm really grateful to my parents, Ferdy and Julia Mount, and my brother and sister, William and Mary Mount.

Thank you very much to Robin Baird-Smith, Gabby Bertin, Mark Bostridge, Chris Bruni-Lowe, David Cameron, Douglas Carswell, Bill Cash, Dominic Cummings, Lindy Dufferin, Matthew Elliott, Nigel Farage, Simone Finn, James Fletcher, Mark Fullbrook, Nick Garland, Michael Gove, Ruth Guilding, Daniel Hannan, Richard Howell, Bernard Jenkin, Boris Johnson, Jo Johnson, Rachel Johnson, Rachel Kelly, Mary Killen, Joshua Levine, Maya and Pankaj Mishra, Archie Mount, Deborah Mount, Francie Mount, Tommy Mount, George Osborne, the late Henrietta Phipps, Tristram and Virginia Powell, Liz Sugg, Gawain Towler, George Trefgarne, Cleo Watson, Molly Watson, A. N. Wilson, Graeme Wilson, Victoria Woodcock and Peter York. Violet Hudson did more than I can ever possibly thank her for.

I'm very grateful, too, to many editors and commissioning editors. They include Paul Dacre, Jennie Agg, Leaf Kalfayan, Peter McKay, Andrew Morrod, Emma Rowley, Andrew Yates and Suzy Walker of the *Daily Mail*, and Laura Freeman, formerly of the *Mail*. Many thanks to Dominic Connolly of the *Mail on Sunday*. Deepest thanks to Andrew Brown, Paul Clements, Rachel Cocker and Charles Moore of the *Daily Telegraph*. I owe a great deal to Sarah Sands and Melanie McDonagh of the *Evening Standard*. Fraser Nelson, Freddy Gray, Emily Hill, Sam Leith, Igor Toronyi-Lalic and Mary Wakefield at *The Spectator* were very kind. Thanks also to Liz Anderson, Alexander Chancellor, Deborah Maby and James Pembroke of *The Oldie*. Many thanks to Martin Ivens, Leaf Arbuthnot, Sarah Baxter, Josh Glancy, Eleanor Mills, Graham Paterson, Laura Pullman and Oliver Thring of the *Sunday Times*. Thanks also to Nancy Sladek of *Literary Review*.

I'm very grateful to Sam Carter for suggesting Biteback as a publisher, and Olivia Beattie as an astonishingly sharp and wise editor. Isabelle Ralphs and James Stephens were publicity whizzes. Peter Straus and Matthew Turner at Rogers, Coleridge & White were lightning quick and planet-brained.

The London Library provided, as always, the best haven in the world.

This book is dedicated to my old tutor, the late Dr Angus Macintyre of Magdalen College, Oxford. When I changed from classics to history, Angus was wonderfully unjudgemental, and so easy-going when I revealed huge gaps in my knowledge. On the night before my Finals, I went to his room in semi-nervous breakdown mode, and he was a reassuring, uplifting, amusing force, as ever. He taught me to realise that history is the best subject of them all.

INDEX